T0065381

The Lord Is My Everything

He Is the Air That I Breathe—Volume III

Day – By – Day

The Holy Ghost Teaches 365 Days a Year

VIVIAN A. NESMITH, M.P.A.

WESTBOW
PRESS®
A DIVISION OF THOMAS NELSON
& ZONDERVAN

This book is a work of non-fiction. Unless otherwise noted, the author and the publisher make no explicit guarantees as to the accuracy of the information contained in this book and in some cases, names of people and places have been altered to protect their privacy.

WestBow Press books may be ordered through booksellers or by contacting:

WestBow Press
A Division of Thomas Nelson & Zondervan
1663 Liberty Drive
Bloomington, IN 47403
www.westbowpress.com
844-714-3454

Because of the dynamic nature of the Internet, any web addresses or links contained in this book may have changed since publication and may no longer be valid. The views expressed in this work are solely those of the author and do not necessarily reflect the views of the publisher, and the publisher hereby disclaims any responsibility for them.

Any people depicted in stock imagery provided by Getty Images are models, and such images are being used for illustrative purposes only. Certain stock imagery © Getty Images.

Scripture taken from the King James Version of the Bible.

ISBN: 978-1-6642-0885-8 (sc)
ISBN: 978-1-6642-0884-1 (hc)
ISBN: 978-1-6642-0886-5 (e)

Library of Congress Control Number: 2018913105

Print information available on the last page.

WestBow Press rev. date: 10/20/2020

This Book Belongs To:

_____

Acknowledgment

In life, we experience the same situations or circumstances; but, we deal with each differently. From the lips of wise women and men, they share golden nuggets or words of wisdom to foster our survival skills. Sowing seeds of wisdom supports increasing areas of our faith in Jesus Christ. The knowledge gained boosts our comprehension. As a result, we can understand how to best deal with a particular circumstance or situation. Often, if one could just simply understand why they must endure such pain, or why on certain days they laugh uncontrollably, or why some days are more energetic than others, maybe everyone could understand how to deal with life in simplicity. However, we fail to understand that life did not come with a manual. Therefore, every circumstance is experiencing the "perils of life," first hand. Growing up, we couldn't wait to become our "own person." It was so important to grow up fast for whatever reasons; that we did not want to take the time to hear and learn from the mistakes made by others. So, we learn from personal failures, what to do differently, and what not to do. Well, trials-and -errors set us back because of poor "listening" skills.

As a child, we depended on others, such as mothers, fathers, grandparents, uncles, aunts, cousins, and the entire family. There was someone that had to teach us how to live. Yet, as we grew, school taught us how to deal with isolated issues relating to life. They explained "How to Become Successful in life," and remained attentive to those that were willing to learn. Somewhere in between the teachings, some pupils fell and became lost in the world. Because so few cared about the lost, so they never made it. You see, there is a difference when we are attentive to wise teachings spoken by wise women and men. You see, in this life, they would have not only spoke on the importance of school but also the importance of serving Jesus Christ.

The wise elders would make an effort to catch the young before their wholly counted out. You would hear words such as, "it is never too late, to get it right, and you still have time." Or maybe, you have listened to, "keep on trusting God, and never give up." These are words that imprint and take charge for a lifetime. Sowing seeds of wisdom not only supports increasing areas of our faith in Jesus Christ, but it also sows seeds of wisdom in the secular bowels of carnal thinking. Hopefully, every soul will take heed to understand and accept Jesus Christ as the "Lord and Savior, The Great Teacher, and Master of All Things.

We acknowledge the godly wisdom of every "Elder" that took the time to share your life's experience and helping to guide our footsteps on the paths of righteousness. For your testimonies have enabled us to become walking epistles of the gospel of truth.

James 1:5
*If any of you lack **wisdom**, let him ask of God, that giveth to all men liberally, and upbraideth not; and it shall be given him.*

Apostle Paul wrote in Hebrews 12:2
Looking unto Jesus the author and finisher of our faith; who for the joy that was set before him endured the cross, despising the shame, and is set down at the right hand of the throne of God.

Always look to Christ for a resolution to all problems. He is the provider and the author of your life's story. As the author, He wrote your life's plan and perfected it according to His will, power, and authority. Hence, without taking a deep breath to reside within His Presence, we falter. Unknowingly, we quietly invite imperfections that sting for a lifetime. Although these faults may appear to overwhelm these vessels of clay, Jesus Christ can perfect all that He has created. As we continue to rehearse the phrase, The Lord is My Everything; He is the air that I breathe. We proclaim total dependence upon our Master. The "One," that has all the power to erase sins.

Often, we lose sight of the things that have a higher value. We have become accustomed to trying to make something fit into nothing. Since Jesus is all so familiar with our mishaps, He is waiting for the opportunity to converse with you. Therefore, the heart must trust and abide by the Book of the Law, treasuring every Word and applying the precepts daily. Know that Righteousness will support growth. But, our Faith will give us the tools for total submission. We as Saints look to Jesus, who is the author and finisher of our faith, and for His wisdom to do what is pleasing unto Him. Although we are called and chosen to share in the gospel, we must mimic the Walk of Jesus Christ and learn of His glory and honor.

The love and kindness that he so willingly portrayed on behalf of a dying world are evidence that we are more than simple creatures. He lovingly breaths upon the frailty of His people and pleads for all to return to Him. God Bless you, look up and live in Jesus' Name.

Contents

Why Are You Tripping

Take Heed and Know Who You Are

Stop Being a Fraidy Cat

The Joint-Heirs

Keep Moving Forward in Boldness

We Are Winners and Never Losers

Keeping It Simple and Sweet

Psalm 119:130

The entrance of thy words giveth light; it
giveth understanding unto the simple.

Keep Fighting

Don't You Dare Faint or Lose

Faith In Jesus Christ

Find the Old Path
The Best Way Is The Lord's Way
Jeremiah 6:16; Acts 5:29; Hebrews 12:14; 1 Corinthians 1:30; Job 8:8; Deuteronomy 32:7

You may have heard it once or twice to "find the old path." As the year's past, we slowly find ourselves derailing from the prospects of righteousness and veering so closely off the path that Christ has set for us. As I look around, there were many things that I saw appeared not out of the norm; but needed a lot more love and caring. Admittedly, we may not have the best of things; but, let's count up the cost for living righteously in the sight of the Living God.

The Children of God have a magnitude and abundance of Jesus Christ's love. For he has granted us the opportunity to seek him for ourselves. Hopefully, we will find him, and after seeing him, we are to take hold of every attribute of faith, courage, hope, trust, and confidence in the majestic powers of Jesus Christ.

It is not easy trying to find the old path. Let us think about it this way. From childhood, you may remember trodden down paths, bare and with very little overgrowth. When we saw a path, we knew it was frequently traveled by many. A well-worn path helps to guide the way to familiar destinations. Grandparents tell stories of trodden down paths and its pitfalls. As a child, I was told to "Find the old path, and it will take you to where you want to go." The overgrowth on the side is boundaries and reminders not to stray from the beaten path. You see, change is scary, and many people are afraid to try new things.

Before planning a road trip, travelers would print out directions, study the maps, program the navigation systems, and familiarize themselves with surrounding areas along the route. If they get lost, sometimes, they will stop, ask for directions, and someone will guide them along the way. So, if you ever get lost traveling on this journey of "Holiness," stop, ask a mighty Christian of valour and honor for guidance. They will lead you in the way of the LORD.

Once you find the old paths – Stand in the ways—as Christians, we must learn the right way to do and say things by showing observance of

1

the commandments, walking in righteousness, living in sanctification and holiness. Try understanding the precepts of holiness by reading and meditating on what is right for your soul. Use your heart to understand and think about what you do before you do it. Recognize the Spirit of God because it is essential to walk in "Holiness."

Some believe Christianity gets bored; but, I tell you this, there is never a dull moment with Jesus Christ. Regularly, learn to communicate with Him. Your deepest secrets are safe with him, and he can erase all your flaws. Finding the Old path does not have to become a tedious journey; Jesus Christ is always full of excitement. Build up your foundation with Him, and he will continue to perfect your life. Take a good long hard look at yourself. What is in your vessel that needs perfecting? Whoever says they are perfect is fooling themselves. Every vessel is tarnished and is desperately in need of polishing. There is so much to do, so recognize your walk and growth in Holiness. Ask for the "old path," Inquire and ask questions to hear their testimony. When we are lost, we ask for direction – It is the path created by The LORD and is according to his Word.

Ask about the former ages

While traveling along the way, ask about the former ages? Ask them, what did they do to remain saved and active in their salvation? The golden age Saints of God would say, "Seek for the right way and ask The LORD how to strengthen your relationship with him." It is easy to go astray. Especially when you are feeling low and discouraged, feelings of loneliness will trick your mind; find ways to keep busy and believe in the Gospel of Truth.

Where Is The Good Way?

The "good way" is a challenge because every day the flesh is warring with the Holy Ghost that is inside you. So, it requires much willpower and faithfulness to remain saved and holy. Protect your SALVATION and love the LORD with your whole heart, body, and soul. Yield everything to Jesus Christ and He will take care of you. Find the Old Path of your elders and learn to worship the LORD Almighty in the beauty of His Holiness.

Find the Old Path, it will lead you into the arms of Jesus Christ. Look at it in this manner, to obey is better than sacrifice. How many times you fall does not count; what is most important is to always get up, repent, and keep on moving forward in Jesus Christ.

Look up and Live!

*You Are Smarter
Than the World*

Um, So What!
Isaiah 65; 2 Corinthians 2; Ephesians 2; Romans 6; Colossians 2

Um, so what! They quote a few scriptures here
and there to challenge your knowledge.

What do you know about God?
What do you know about Jesus?
What do you know about anything?
What can you tell me?
Tell me something I do not know?

Hurling questions one after another is a tactic to mask bruised emotions, trapped behind the walls of pain and discomfort. In their hearts, some may wonder why they are at the bottom and not the top. Distress and embarrassment harden the heart of the lost. Regardless of the numerous efforts to share the good news of Jesus Christ, their heart is not ready to receive what God has prepared for them that loves Him.

Brokenness dismantles relationship barriers and interferes with healing and deliverance. They have not learned and do not know how to surface and receive the clean air of the Holy Ghost. A breeze blown from the lips of Our Savior could easily erase the pain. I believe it, and someone might call me crazy. People are lost and hurting from past afflictions, which has seeped into the current state of mind.

Um, So, what, let them yell! Miserable souls cry out in despair. They are filled with contention and babbling arguments without a cause. You are in the hand of Jesus Christ, keep your mind focused on what is good and profitable to the soul. Showering thoughts of love, singing sweet melodies, filling your heart with harmony beats of praises. The lost are blindfolded by mischievous acts which are holding them captive and bond.

In these things, you are smarter than the world. The Lord Jesus Christ has changed your entire wardrobe and name. You are sanctified, freed from sin, and is now the servant of righteousness. Do not look upon their lowliness. Encourage them from afar and continue speaking the truth in love. If you show pity, you might win them over because you kept the unity of the Spirit in the bonds of peace.

The Lord has transformed your heart and mind. Therefore, you must mirror holiness; continue to let the word of God manifest by the scriptures according to His commandments and everlasting love. Even in times of slothfulness, keep laboring in the vineyard and keep it simple for others to understand until they come in the fullness of the blessings of the gospel Jesus Christ. Let us walk honestly before Him as epistles sharing stories filled with experience. Testify to all who listens! Tell them you have tasted God's grace and are walking in the newness of life.

You are smarter than the world! Now you are unto God a sweet savour of Christ, faithful to the saved and unsaved. Yet, the World is withering away in sinful deeds of trivial riddles and dreadful giggles. As they gaze upon the new you, envy feels their hearts; yearning to know how you got the glorious glow.

A simple inquiry here and there could lead them directly to the place of prayer. It is easy as one, two, and three; personal iniquities blindside them, knocking them to their knees. So, what, let them talk, keep strutting, and walk the talk. Turn around, let them see what a beautiful soul brand new and clean.

Um, so what! Let them quote a few scriptures here and there at least you know they care. Lost souls too afraid to return home and receive God's grace. It is okay for a short while when you see them smile. You are no longer a stranger in this land, but fellow-citizens and a Saint in the household of God. As a result, you have learned how to build and construct a frame designed to grow in the Holy Ghost and become a temple in the LORD.

You are smarter than the World, a beautiful pearl. Smooth all around, let their transgressions label them as a clown. Move a little more to the right and let them see. Jesus Christ controls your life; tell all—spread the Word, give the testimonies, and watch them flee. Be cautious and gentle; do not fret because if you do, they will see you as a threat. A threat to their kingdom of nothings surrounded with cussing and fussing. It is not a peaceful place, and even they need grace.

Grace to heal, fill, and appeal. Lead them closer with a smile and uphold your new lifestyle. We were alienated from Jesus Christ by the uncircumcision of our flesh. It was quickened together with Jesus Christ, and he forgave us for all our trespasses. His blood blotted out the handwritten ordinances that were against us. He took it away and nailed it to his cross.

A new life, wearing new clothes and walking in a new pair of shoes. Did you tell them, "You are smarter than the World?" Please show them your new shoes. It came with new clothes and a new attitude. The conversations are Yay and Nay, conversing in holy gossip using seasoned words, fit for the Child of a Living King.

No fancy colors, just pure white will do; soon, they will want the same as you. Walk slow and not too fast. Take time to enjoy the fruit of your labor; remember to love those mean, selfish neighbors. Understand you are the salt of the earth; do not lose your usefulness.

Um, so what! Let them vainly puff up their fleshly minds. Let them quote their scriptures here, there, and everywhere. You are useful and necessary. Show them you care about their broken lives and say a prayer. You are smarter than the World. A light of comfort in difficult times stands high on the hilltop and spread the Gospel of Truth nonstop.

You are smarter than the World because you returned home to Jesus Christ, Lord, and Savior. Um, so what! Let them quote their scriptures here, there, and everywhere. Smile and to show you care. You are smarter than the World. Never feed into the dream world; reality is real, and Jesus Chris operates the Potter's wheel. Let them know young and old; Jesus Christ can make them whole.

Why Tithe
Haggai 1; Malachi 3:8-10; Leviticus 27:31

Christians struggle with trying to maintain their identity. Pretenders or fake Christians do not put forth the effort in trying to uphold their integrity. Instead, many purposely continue to wobble in their walk. Yes, it requires hard work and persistence with remaining obedient. Every day, the world intimidates Christianity, whereas some feel they cannot live up to its interpretation of success. Society trips up our demeanor and attacks our character as if we cannot comprehend its strategy. As a result, Christians become so entangled with life's necessities they forget about trusting Jesus Christ to make provisions.

For instance, when I was a single mother, the world (unsaved); saw me as a weak sheep. My appearance did not look like that of a King's daughter. Instead, it resembled desperation and poverty. And my family's daily necessities remained unmet, and my children were looking to me when the utilities were disconnected. At some point, I had to stop and think about my position in Jesus Christ. Yes, I was saved and still had the mentality for occasional sin. I knew Jesus Christ, accepted Him as my everything; yet, it was a struggle for me. I needed that one-on-one training on "How to Become A Servant of God."

One day, "The Holy Ghost" instructed me to give my full paycheck as tithe and offering. I was already in a bind and living from paycheck to paycheck. At the time, my bi-weekly earnings of $750 did not relieve my debts. Besides, obedience is better than any sacrifice. So, I gave the entire check as a tithe, and offering. Since then, Jesus Christ has met my family's basic needs.

What happens if you find yourself in a bind or the expenses incurred in the household are more than the check? Well, I am glad you asked. It is a trick of the enemy to test your confidence and faithfulness in Jesus Christ. If you find yourself in a situation where you think to no longer give tithes and offerings, please stop and think about your current situation and what you have to lose? Remember, the Lord is Jehovah Jireh, and he will provide your every need. At times it may seem as if you cannot attain or sustain your home. But you have the power to control your spending habits. I know we all like nice things and love to pay ourselves for working hard to earn a check. However, we must think about the love and kindness of Jesus Christ. We must do our part to help take care of the House of God and not neglect the needs of the Church. When you look for much, and it came to little; and when you brought it home, The LORD blows upon it. Why? Because the House of God goes neglected or without, and we run every man to his own house to take care of its needs.

The LORD only requires us to give ten percent of our **GROSS**, not the **NET EARNINGS**. Jesus Christ has provided us the jobs to earn wages to take care of our home. As a result, he is only asking for 10% of our earnings. Regardless make an effort to trust that he can sustain you and your family. All Saints of God are encouraged to tithe irrespective of how the finances may look in the home. So many falter in tithing, while others omit giving it for a short time. On a few occasions, I did not give tithes or an offering. I allowed simple necessities to interrupt my confidence in Jesus Christ. The bills kept coming, and the pressure was mounting, and I felt trapped and did not know how to get back into the rhythm of giving.

Thus, I found myself not walking as a faithful servant. My soul did not find rest, for my thoughts were ever so focused on bill collectors, groceries, and etcetera. Small things such as daily necessities could quickly shift your focus in another direction. Debts are distractions of the heart because the mind is not focusing on the good way. One day, after Church, I went to my mentor, who is one of the Pastors, to ask for guidance. His reply was simple and straightforward, "repent and resume giving your tithe."

When you start to tithe, do not think about what the church leadership does with the money. It no longer concerns you; let God deal with them if they do not do what they are supposed to do concerning the monetary gifts of the House of God. Only Jesus Christ has the authority to chastise the Church Leadership. Their behavior is between them and the Lord, our God. I have heard so many people speak up against church leaders and their financial management skills. The heresies focused intensely on how the Church was spending the funds; some members left and refused to return.

What we do as Children of God is making an effort to obey the scriptures. Our focus is to find favor in the eyesight of God and not man. We are not man pleasures, but worshippers of Jesus Christ. Focus on what is required of you according to the word of God. Jesus Christ takes care of those that are obedient to his commandments. He will keep you in good health, prosperity, and your soul will prosper in him. It is not always about the monetary value, or it is not still about how much money you have in your pocket.

It is the prosperity of the gifts of the Holy Ghost and the joy. Children of God can prosper in other ways as well; do not forget we also flourish in the spiritual and in the natural or physical. Take your eyes off man and focus on the things of God. If you are so worried about how the church is spending the money, then you should remove yourself from the more prominent churches and find a smaller church to attend. It takes a great deal of money to operate a large church than it is to run a smaller church. You pay for the amenities offered by the church, and some Churches work with full staff, making it more of a business. If you cannot afford to hang with the big names, find your way and hang out with the smaller. At my Church, we do not have financial problems.

From one Saint to another, give your tithes and offering and trust in Jesus Christ to meet your every need. For the earth is the Lord's and the fullness thereof and all that dwell in it. He is faithful to his promises.

Perfecting Your Servanthood in Jesus Christ

Obedience, Righteousness, Sanctification, and Holiness are characterized as you grow in Jesus Christ. Four simple words require so much attention and hard work to build and stand on. One-on-One interaction with and in the Holy Ghost will teach you "How To Become A Servant of God." The more you submit to reading the Word of God, then you will find yourself in between each page of the Bible. Commitment produces righteousness, sanctification, and holiness because you will begin to understand servanthood, and your willpower will increase towards obedience.

Apostle Paul reminds us that "we ought to obey God rather than men." It goes to say, trust God in and with all things. We are peculiar people that receive peculiar favors from a Peculiar God. Stand in the ways of righteousness, and when you are lost, ask a faithful servant for the old path and the good way. There in the presence of God, you will find rest for your soul.

Other necessary strong qualities are sanctification and holiness. We are a part of the Body of Christ; as such, we are in Christ Jesus, and He is made of God to us *wisdom, righteousness, sanctification, and redemption.* For better judgment, Christians should desire wisdom; it will help to minimize ignorance and increases our perception towards Holiness. Our living in *sanctification* requires complete separation, consecration, and omission from sins. We trick ourselves by iniquities while entangled in bondage. Do not allow the deceptive ways of friends and family to persuade your walk in Jesus Christ. It is so easy to lose track of your salvation, and the world does not have sympathy for no one.

We deprive ourselves of the gifts that bring forth good by embracing the corrupt nature of folly. Jesus Christ is made righteousness for our souls, and we can effectually seek after redemption and trust that He will redeem us. Because holiness without which no man will see the Lord. Take heed to your relationship and walk behind the LORD of your salvation.

What is in your vessel that needs perfecting. Every temple is tarnished and is desperately in need of polishing. When we are lost, we ask for direction. Hence, ask about the former ages. Ask a committed Christian how they were able to walk upright in the presence of Jesus Christ. Hopefully, you will hear them say that they made it through by obedience, faith, trust, and confidence in the LORD. Enquire at the hand of God for directions to the Throne of Grace. Humbly lay at His feet and tarry there for the unction of the Holy Ghost. Perfect your servanthood in Jesus Christ, preparing yourself to search for His wisdom daily.

Enquire and ask, "What did they do to remain saved and active in their salvation?" Seek the right way and perfect your faults by refining your appetite for holiness. Christians should desire to live according to the biblical principles outlined in all the books of the Bible. It is easy to go astray and hard to get back, but not impossible. There will come times where you may feel discouraged; never lose faith in who you are and ask another committed Christian how to strengthen your relationship with Jesus Christ. Their answer should always revert you to the biblical practices of obedience, sanctification, holiness, and redemption. Believe in the Gospel of Truth, which God's way.

Do you remember when you first received Jesus Christ as your Lord and Savior? Consider the years of many generations and how many before you walked. Some fainted along the way, while others kept moving with perseverance, power, and strength. Ask your Father, Jesus Christ, and he will show you how to achieve greatness in Him. Ask the elders, and they may say, "the challenge is to remain saved and holy." Walk therein, walk upright before the LORD, and you will find rest for your soul. When you run into the few who have fainted, and they say "they will not walk therein," for the sake of your salvation, separate yourself. Continue to practice sanctification and keep it moving.

A Good Life Is Being Married To Jesus Christ

Ezekiel 24

Life is filled with different types of aches and pains. Sometimes it has bad days, and some days are hard and cruel. How we handle the curveballs it throws depends on our relationship in Jesus Christ. The LORD molded and fashioned us in His image, which is perfect and pure. Life was spoken and given as an everlasting gift. If you desire to embrace it, reshape it to reflect the principles of holiness. Unlike our clothes, which we change according to our likes, dislikes, and fashion trends, we decide the style. There are things that we can change, and many we cannot. We can spruce it up, camouflage it, mix or match, make it simple, create a positive look, or pretend to appear strong like a superhero, or poor and undesirable. Deep within, the soul feels weak because it's traumatized from the ailments of life. Argue your point and stand up when you feel powerful and secure. If you choose a plain and simple life, at least try tailoring it with ornaments or richness and grace. Jesus Christ gave us life as a token of love from the Father.

We are empty shells ready to be filled with good things to make us noticeable. As the Word of God ministers to our heart, it takes root and slowly manifests on the inside. Patiently, we wait for it to unravel, transforming our outer appearance. Until then, we lay at the feet of Jesus Christ, with pangs and sorrows as the bread of tears run down like a river day and night.

It is easier to blame others for the hardships in life. To resolve the issues, have you ever stopped to think, retreat, and take a different approach? Physically, we wipe tears away with our fingers, tissue, or a small cloth. If left to dry, the tears will stain the face. It does not matter, because the heart is agitated by failures. Spiritually, those tears leave stains that scars our faith, and these stains require a more loving approach. Hence, with a stroke of His finger, the Lord, takes away the desire to cry; neither will your tears run down. Life is never fair; but, it is your choice to serve the Lord with all humility of mind. Travail against emerging temptations, vexation of spirit, and satisfy your soul with the richness of peace.

Guilt stained tears are removed through repentance, the honesty of heart, and truth. Every tear stain has its own story, and we know them to be expected because and they exist from life struggles. You know life is what we make it. The beauty of life is what it is. It is formulated and calculated by experience and our actions. We have stories to share to make others laugh or cry. Or maybe they are simple stories possibly rumored from here to there.

A good life is being married to Jesus Christ. Some people treasure marriage, while others struggle to keep it together. If you sit back and think about it, the marriage of Jesus Christ and the backsliders are unforgettable love stories. In parts of the world, marriage consists of one husband and many wives. According to the Word, Old Testament, we have read of those having multiply wives to include concubines. In the New Testament, marriage consists of one wife and one husband. It is not about cultural differences; but more about values. How can a married couple, which is biblically defined as a marriage between a man and woman, desire more than what is natural and required? I do believe it to be true, whereas you love one and hate the other. Secular values are contaminated and confusing.

Life is like a marriage entwined with Grace from a loving husbandman. Who loves unconditionally, soothes the pain where it hurts most, makes you smile for no reason at all, Whispers in your ear the good things that help you to stand strong, teaches you how to fight, while He's winning battles, and remains true to His every Word. He speaks up for you, when you are right and defends you when others say you are wrong. He requires you to hold your peace, and he will fight your battles. A husbandman that takes you back without questions. He requires you to ask forgiveness, turn away, and sin no more. A good life is being married to Jesus Christ and making every effort to honor your vows as well as those He created.

Obedience Knows Wisdom
Mark 4:1-9; Romans 16; 2 Corinthians 7:15;
Psalm 25:12; Proverbs 14; Proverbs 15

The parable spoken by Jesus Christ symbolizes the simplicity with understanding the Word of God. It is defined throughout his doctrine how to live and create a life that represents our true colors while maintaining truthfulness. As we teach His doctrine, each precept should be pleasant to the ear so that the heart can receive it. When we understand what someone is asking us to do, it is taking in stride, and efforts are initiated to perfect it.

The balancing factor is receiving and hearing, which is activated when you tap into your "Spiritual Receptivity." Every person responds to the Word of God differently. Some take the Word of God as affirmation; thus, applying it to a certain issue. Others harden their hearts, refusing to receive the Oracles of God because of their dislike for the Vessel (person), presenting the message. Often, these are the people who show up to Church every Sunday and are distractions to the listeners. Then, you have a few who allow the Word of God to take root in their hearts. Afterward, they wait on it to manifest and continue living according to biblical principles.

Devoted Saints knows obedience is better than sacrifice and the fear of the Lord is the beginning of knowledge. In contrast, a foolish person despises wisdom and instruction. The Gospel of Truth is made to manifest by the scriptures of the prophets, according to the commandment of the everlasting God. His Word is made known to all for the obedience of faith.

Hence, Christ took the time to distinguish between those who must feast on milk versus those that eat meat. Those requiring milk still need someone to nourish their Faith, support their growth, and lead by example. Jesus spoke with many parables as he gave the word to all willing to hear. Only Jesus can increase your understanding as well as your knowledge. Obedience knows wisdom because the person who is willing to give it their all towards receiving the Word of God; desires to draw nearer to Him. Having a fear of the Lord strengthens confidence: and in Him, you can find a place of refuge.

Having Faith and Confidence

Sometimes, a boost is needed to push a person a little further into the Will of God. It gives them the confidence to know they can trust in the invisible things of God. The world thinks we are crazy because we worship a God we cannot see. Their small little minds and cluttered hearts do not see Jesus Christ in the beauty of His holiness. If they knew of our struggles, possibly, they might be willing to understand the pains, and their perspective will be a lot different.

As you embark on your journey, there are a few loose ends to tie together. One end is acknowledging obedience is the fountain of life. Having confidence in yourself and the uprightness of your ways depends on your fear and hope in Jesus Christ. His grace will bring you through hard tribulations. So, continue to learn obedience and stop tripping over your feet because you do not know how to stand up without falling. Can you sit still for a second or two? Let your obedience be visible to those you know to include family and friends. For the Lord will ask that we be wise onto that which is good, and simple concerning evil. Never let your guard down, but remaining alert to distractions and troubles.

Christ in His affection is more abundant toward us because he remembers the obedience of all His people. So, have confidence in your obedience, knowing that you will do what is required of you. Choose to serve God in the sanctification of the Spirit, which helps to anchor your belief. Gather your hearts together, with the sprinkling of the blood of Jesus Christ, his grace brings peace, and it will multiply. As you mature in the Word of God, the Lord has foreknowledge of your future, and He is willing to guide you into what is good and acceptable through your faith in Him.

What is Wisdom
James 1; Psalm 111; Proverbs 1; Proverbs 2; Proverbs 3

The fear of the Lord is the beginning of wisdom, and those who gain good understanding obey the commandments of God, and his praise endures forever. Wisdom is given to steer us in the right direction, awaken, and sharpen our judgment. If any is lacking Wisdom, ask for her, and he will give to all men liberally and upbraided not; and it will be given.

Wisdom is crying in the streets for the folly of humanity abandoned her. Who wants to share the wealth of knowledge she desires to give? She was present in the beginning when God, The Father, created the earth and established the heavens. Only the Lord could give us the wisdom to help us understand how to obey and keep His Law. With wisdom, we could gain strength, receive counsel, and understanding from the Holy Ghost who instructs us to depart from iniquities. So, we incline our ears to hear her speak and take wisdom to heart and apply and understanding. Building a relationship with Wisdom, she comforts the heart, gives knowledge, and is pleasant to the soul. Wisdom enhances our ears to hear the spoken oracles and statues of holiness. Study and learn to do what is good and let your speech be seasoned and of good report.

Wisdom will help us to maintain our relationship and communion with The LORD Jesus Christ. She will teach us how to worship and acknowledge His presence. Our increased knowledge of Him becomes evident in the lifestyles lived. Children of God must know how to conduct themselves according to learned biblical principles. Practice wisdom by justly meditating on the scriptures and allowing the Holy Ghost to perfect your temple.

Forsaking wisdom makes knowledge and understanding void. Without her, you cannot receive revelation and will find it challenging to comprehend the Gospel of Truth. True wisdom is manifested through, and the Holy Ghost who teaches all things, and bring all things to remembrance, whatsoever Our Lord and Savior have said. Take hold of Wisdom and let her not go for she is your life and will preserve your ways. Her instruction will not let you turn aside for her duty is to stay on the path of righteousness. Sound wisdom will uphold your integrity while increasing confidence in your salvation, faith, and trust in Jesus Christ.

Stand Tall and Pay Attention

The Mind Never Sleeps

Jeremiah chapter 4:14; Jeremiah 29:11; Isaiah chapter 59:7; Romans 12:1-2; 1 Peter 2:5; Romans 6:13; Proverbs 3; Philippians 4; Psalm 121

I read an article that says the mind never sleeps. It was a bit puzzling because the LORD says he gives His beloved sweet sleep. When we lie down, be not afraid because our sleep should be sweet. The conscience is clear, free from disturbance, and sudden fears. Somehow, we disturb our peace with vain thoughts having no value. The mind may never sleep; but, God's Children have learned to bring every evil imagination into captivity and every thought to the obedience of Jesus Christ.

A mind that never sleeps is plotting wickedness. The heart, mind, and soul communicate together enjoining vain thoughts of rejection and stressful situations which disturbed its sleep. There is no rest for weary souls which trembles at fiend mountains and enraging fears. Sitting still, pondering on acts of revenge destroys our faith. It is time wasted thinking on the affairs of life and feasting on displeasures that diminish your self-worth. Cast down imaginations and every high thing that exalts itself against the knowledge of God. Wake up in your Spirit and allow it to rest on the things of God. Think on these things, whatsoever things are true. You cannot win the battles in your thoughts; but God has the power to control your mind. Learn to plead the blood of Jesus over your head and think about things that are true to the gospel and real to you. Whatsoever things are honest because the truth will never change.

The mind never sleeps because we waste so much time thinking about ways to resolve the problem and towards the end we are without the answer. Be honest with yourself and identify your strengths and weaknesses. Do not allow foolish behavior to ruin your salvation. Think on whatsoever things are pure and satisfying to your soul. Think on whatsoever things are lovely; for pleasant thoughts could change your perspective on the situation. Think on whatsoever things are of good report; if there be any virtue, and if there be any praise, think on these things. Good reports are victorious battles won by Our Lord and Savior.

When victory reigns, praises ring throughout the land. Celebrations break forth like a sunny day without the rain clouds.

Someone wrote an article, that the mind never sleeps. Some say that we train it to think about the past and present. We cling to painful memories and traumatic experiences; refusing to let go. So, the mind never sleeps because it is replaying those occurrences while you are resting. How often do we train it to remember the importance of pleasing and maintaining the laws of righteousness and the word of God? Probably, not at all. It is busy racing against time revolting against deliverance and healing.

Does the mind have the capabilities to hold such knowledge and bring to us-ward the profitable things of God? Our little minds can only remember so much and most of the time we forget. The elderly can remember the past, present, and speak about the future. They sleep and rise early; not missing a beat in their routines. Yet, somehow, the younger generation holds to impure and vengeful thoughts. Easily they toss away peace and goodwill. Their minds never sleep because of chaotic circumstances, revengeful acts, deceitful plots, angering moments, and jobless attitudes. They sleep and rise late; having not a routine to entertain their thoughts. As a result, many fall prey to social norms of loafing; free-riding on the attempts of others.

The mind never sleeps because we fill it with improper thoughts and challenging images painted by daily struggles. The mind never sleeps; and The LORD never sleeps nor slumber. He continues to observe the good, bad, as well as our uncertainties. We can find sweet sleep by lifting our eyes unto the hills, from which comes our help. Know, your help comes from the LORD, which made the heaven and earth. He knows the thoughts we think, and the memories stored. Nothing is hid from Him and nothing is ignored. Despite the trial, if you only trust in Him, he will not suffer your foot to be moved. You do not have to worry, scheme, or devise foolish acts which may topple your salvation. Even as you dream, He is watchful and never weary. Scientifically, it may be true that the mind never sleeps. Spiritually, God is in control and captivates the thoughts of his sheep trading them for thoughts of peace.

Your Thoughts Are Void Without The Word of God
1 Chronicles chapter 28:9, Micah 4:12; 2 Corinthians 10:5; Jeremiah 7; Galatians 6; Ephesians 2

Many refuse to sit still and apply or meditate on the Word of God. They refuse to understand the slothfulness which has prevented growth in their spiritual body. The Lord understands the mind, and graciously controls it. If he does not regulate the mind, many of us would probably lose it.

Lose our train of thought,
lose our memories,
lose our purpose,
lose the sense of direction,
lose our identity,
lose our place in life—and etcetera.

A wondering mind is empty and void. Take time and think on the Word of God, read a scripture or two and think about the message the Holy Ghost is relaying. Transform your mind to be in the perfect will of God by simply meditating on what is right and comforting to the Soul. Do not give yourself over to sin. Instead, know who you are and resist the devil by developing an obedience to Christ Jesus. Casting down imaginations, and every high thing that exalts itself against the knowledge of God. Your thoughts are void without the Word of God because we are slacking with our covenant. Search your thoughts? When was the last time you fasted? Or the last time you sat and read for at least an hour? Sit down and think of the last time you went to the altar and tarried there and waited for God to answer?

Listen Friend, recuperate, regroup, and start anew. Clear your mind by going for a walk. You do not have to go far; around the corner or in your neighborhood is fine. I learned from a Pastor to go and sit by the water and talk with the LORD. Tell him about the good and bad;

converse with him as if you are talking to a friend. He is listening and attentive to your requests. Find a quiet place, journal down your thoughts, talk to God, and find a simple stress releaser to empty your mind. Bring into captivity every thought to the obedience of Christ; through fasting and praying. Do not reject what is of God but strive for holiness. You cannot walk according to the word unless you believe. Believe he hears you when you call and do according to what the Lord says.

At times, you may get weary in well doing; in due season you will reap, if you faint not. Continue to do what is required of you, shake off the hardship and lay aside every weight that so easily beset you. Life chastises in many ways, but Jesus Christ has the power and resolution for the storm. If you do not read or study to show yourself approved unto God, a workman that need not to be ashamed, rightly dividing the word of truth. Your thoughts are void without the Word of God. Transform your mind and listen. Neither incline your ear, to unwise counsel from the ungodly. The word of God is quick and powerful, to strengthen our faith, that we may obtain this rest. Jesus Christ is quick to judge in all efforts of disobedience by encouraging the Saints to imprint the Word of God on the heart and remain conscience of their deeds. It is vital to live according to the Holy Ghost and receive the power to pull down the strong holds of the enemy. God's Word cuts both the Saint and sinner uprooting sinful habits, converting souls, bringing hearts, and minds into subjection to His Will. The sword which is the Word of God divides between the joints and the marrow, searching the most secret, parts of the soul. Let the Holy Ghost, who is the discerner of our thoughts and heart, help to build up your profession of faith in him.

The Gospel of Peace
Ephesians 6:10-20; Ephesians 5; Romans 10; Corinthians 13; Philippians 4

The preparation of the gospel of peace will defend your spiritual walk. It helps you to abide by the gospel and walk according to the Commandments of God. Gospel peace is defined as having personal peace, spiritual peace, and charitable peace. Your shield of faith should believe in the characteristics of Jesus, in the purpose of the gospel, and in yourself.

The sword of the Spirit and Salvation strengthens our hope, perseverance, and helps us build faith. Jesus Christ loves us and gave himself for the Church, so we can be sanctified and cleansed with the washing of water by the word. He has the power to present us without a spot, or wrinkle, or any such thing. His people must be holy and without blemish.

Spiritual maturity is trusting you can stand without wavering in your faith, but emulating the attributes of peace. When you were a child, you spoke as a child, understood as a child, and thought as a child. When you became older, you put away childish things and desired a change reflecting Jesus Christ. We have to preach the gospel of peace and bring glad tidings of good things.

We have hidden the word of God in the heart to preserve our soul. Pray always in all types of holy prayers and supplications. Make known your request in the Spirit, watching while having perseverance and making supplication for all. Pray always for peace, and on all occasions, keep up your disposition in the Holy Ghost. It gives utterance when we do not know what to pray or say. We understand the issues of life flows from the heart. However, we must be attentive to the needs of others and apply prayer to resolve all situations. The peace of God passes all understanding, should keep your hearts and minds through Christ Jesus.

Promise Keeper
Hebrew 12; Isaiah 55; John 3

Jesus is the author and finisher of our faith. He wrote out a life plan and perfected it according to his will, power, and authority. Only he can provide corrective direction that is necessary for the growth of all called and chosen by him.

The love and kindness that he so willingly portrayed on the cross is evidence of who we are to him. Jesus Christ determines our faith and re-defines our character. Look onto Him, who is the judge, rewarder, and promise keeper.

For God so loved the world, that he gave his only begotten Son, that whosoever believes in him should not perish, but have everlasting life. He saved us, paid the price for our sinful ways, and gave us life in abundance. He is a promise keeper; His Word is true. Have you sat and thought of all that has taken place over the years? Now, evaluate your current position? If you are sensitive to the Holy Ghost, your eyes may have teared up a little. Jesus Christ is a Promise Keeper to those who are obedient to his commandments and follow his path. Once his Word goes forth out of His mouth, it will not return unto Him void, but it will accomplish that which He please, and it will prosper in the thing whereto He sent it.

Think hard, The Father, Son, and Holy Ghost have never forsaken His sheep. He has kept his promises from Genesis to Revelations. Maybe, there were moments of confusion and despair; and we had no idea what He was doing at a "particular moment." When you come to the time of peace and rest; then you can hear the Holy Ghost. Find your quiet spot, search your inward man, rest your thoughts, and think on the wonderful acts which Jesus Christ has performed for you.

Won't He Do It and Did He Do It!

He is a PROMISE KEEPER

Frailty
Psalm 39; Romans 8

The chastisement of God crushes the morality of flesh. It interferes with the holy will of God and his word which encourages trust. See the outcome with an eye of faith knowing that God in his sovereignty and dominion has all power. We are given the freedom and will to seek the Lord in times of stress. Without God there is nothing; everything said or done is all in vanity. Without Him, flesh has no strength to stand firm on it is own. For the Lord is the founder and keeper; it is he that designed our purpose and enlightens our understanding. Hence, we are cannot stand strong without his strength and power.

The enemy will devour us whole and the double-minded hearts are traps set for destruction. We are compassed about by many witnesses that testifies of lustful desires and frailty to stand. Our feeble knees are not strong enough to stand against the enemy because of the burdens that weighs heavily on the shoulders of God's people.

We have the power to release the heavy loads and retain our relationship with Jesus Christ. The LORD makes us to know our end, and the measure of our days, what it is that we may know how frail we are because of the carnality of our thinking. Instead of choosing to please God, we desire to feed our appetite for sin. Occasional sins, we believe others will not know; but God knows them all. Amid the frailty and our inability to stand alone; we depend upon the Holy Ghost to help with our infirmities.

As we meet God at the altar, or the place chosen for prayer; we begin to search our hearts for the right words to say. For we know not what we should pray or what we ought to pray. With a sincere heart, call upon the Name of Jesus, tarry for a little while and wait for the Holy Spirit to make intercession for you with groanings which cannot be uttered.

He makes it known to the Father what is hidden deeply in the heart. Jesus Christ understands all things. Never let your frailties or infirmities prevent you from getting up. If you fall, do not sit there and die spiritually. Repent, Get up, and Get moving.

The Barren
Matthew 21; Mark 11; Nehemiah 1; Psalm 92

Many are called, ordained, sent by the father, and later withers away? They wither away in devotion because they could not handle the depressing and scolding comments. The scolding's test your relationship with Jesus Christ. After years attending Church and working in ministry; you begin to have second thoughts. Therefore, you ask yourself a series of questions.

Self, and Self answers "Huh," and you ask:
"Did I make the right move?"
"Did Jesus Christ call me?"
"Or, did I call myself?"
"Can I walk worthy of the vocation which I am called?"

Know this, you are worthy and take the calling serious. Regardless, how you may feel, clearly understand your duty. Consider what Jesus Christ has done for you and to what purpose he has called you. Now, live up to your profession and calling. The grace of God has prepared and made you acceptable to the gospel by which you are called. Walking in your vocation means to be called; therefore, you must answer and observe your vow. Do not allow skepticism to wear down Faith. If so, resentment will pin you in the corner of defeat and uncertainty will cloud your judgement. Thus, destroying your Faith one truth at a time. The truth which is the belief in The Father, Son, and Holy Ghost.

Those second thoughts will be invaded with additional questions without merit to your purpose. None of it has any value; but you cannot understand or see the conversion; because of the fogged vision. The mind is flooded with many possibilities: Maybe, the praise was not loud enough. Or, possibly the prayer not sincere enough. Could it be the worship was not real enough? Oh, yeah this is it; maybe I soared so high, got a little dizzy and begin to faint.

Remain focused. Do not lose ground or your grip in securing confidence in Jesus Christ. Workers of iniquity repeatedly challenges the hearts and mind of God's people. They have nothing better to do;

but, to torment and distract the servants of Jesus Christ. You would not notice it because you are to busy fainting, sliding deep into the pit of sorrow and disdain. The adversary has weighed upon your shoulders until you refuse to stretch forth your hands for help because of pride. Pride wins nothing and continuously loses because of its thirst for dignity and embarrassment to ask for help. Sometimes, it is okay to ask for help in times of weakness. No one expects you to do everything alone. You do not want to let anyone down; so, what do you do when a group is tearing you down with envy.

They envy the labor, devotion to the ministry, and your brethren; they are suffering as well. So, the workers of iniquity know they are strong at destroying the good work God has started within His servants. After hearing our Senior Pastor teach on guarding the Word of God in our heart; its understood to hold on to the teachings and never let the adversary attack your spiritual morals. It is hard trying to live holy let alone having someone constantly berate and not build up. It is like tearing down your Spiritual Self-Esteem, ignoring the anointing placed on your head, and the Blood that washed away the mistakes and sins. Workers of iniquity does not want to look beyond your faults and refuse to release past mistakes of others in fear of not having leverage.

The Barren must stop and think about being in the right place at the right time for Jesus Christ to fix whatever is broken in their life. Stop letting the opinions of others traumatize your Spiritual Growth. You cannot draw any nutrients from bad substances. They cannot fertile the fruit of the Spirit because they are not abiding in the true vine which is Jesus Christ. Thus, they miss the opportunity to experience Him in the beauty of holiness. Too much time is spent in watching others and not watching God. When the Word of God is heard, they become immature listeners, neglecting the truth, and not perceiving the meaning of the Gospel of Truth. They have their meaningless interpretation, which causes them to suffer in trying times.

When you feel naked, but seeking to be adorned by God's presence, you must put in the work to seek the good things. Salvation is "FREE," but, Saints of God must work to create a FAITH-BASED relationship far beyond simple. Create a masterpiece! Although Jesus Christ knows you by name; you want a name flashing in neon lights and bursting fireworks.

Well, maybe not so drastic—okay, how about a whining baby crying loudly. Hannah cried and prayed within herself. The LORD heard and received the sincerity of her heartfelt prayer. Well, my mouth is big and loudly cry like a baby. So, it takes all the above and more.

Think about it, when there is a competitive event, the participants work to make themselves stand out. Regardless, you will remember the competitor by the best or worst presentations. Well, I need the neon lights and bursting fireworks. Some things require His immediate attention. We must find our niche in gaining the attention of Jesus Christ.

The barren is a dry season and a desolate moment in time. Remember, somethings come forth by nothing, but by prayer and fasting. When your soul is in great affliction and reproach, turn to fasting, and praying before the God of heaven. He is surely attentive to the call of them who observe his commandments. In prayer, acknowledge who he is, confess your sins, and then make the petitions and supplications known. Never give up, fight the fight of faith, remain planted in the house of the LORD. Those that be planted in the house of the LORD will flourish in His courts. He continues to plant, water, and promote people willing to share the Gospel. Who is barren amongst the heathen and is willing to go forth as predestined from long ago. Many of his children are desolate and unfruitful in the knowledge of our Lord Jesus Christ.

He is the hedge of protection set for around to protect and keep. He sent them out to share, preach, and teach all nations. When it was their time to serve within the body or ministry of Christ the world entrapped them in the affairs of the wicked; and beat his people daily. He continues to send forth his messengers to share the good news of the Gospel. Still, they receive them not, but continue casting stones, confusing the mind, and sending them down to shame. The Lord continues to send his people into a world full of generational vipers, who is ready to kill, beat, and destroy the purpose. Instead of the servants of God presenting themselves strong, rooted, and grounded they show up vulnerable. Fear has caused their feeble bodies to reject the purpose causing the infirmities of the wicked to refuse Salvation. Receive the Word of the living God. He sent his only son Jesus Christ for the world to reverence and uphold his name. The world plotted to destroy the cornerstone of our temple and failed.

The arrogance and intimidation from society should not become an excuse for not fulfilling works of the ministry. If Moses would have allowed a speech impairment to stop him from accomplishing his work; he would have missed a great opportunity. He would not have experienced the Omnipotence of the Lord God. Let us not forget the obedience of Samuel. When the Lord chose him to the office of a prophet, had his mother not kept her vow, God's people may have been without an overseer to encourage them.

What great works he have accomplished for the kingdom of God? In perilous times of old God's people suffered many hardships. How many were barren and refused to obey the call to fulfill their strength. Ignore talks against the ministry and the infirmities of God's people. Servants of God continue to turn away in fear even after reading of their predecessors written on the pages of Bible. The pages share stories of those who fulfilled their duties and the obedience of others. So, answer your call into Ministry. You are barren and the time is now to birth the gift of the Spirit. Do not be afraid to move forward in what you know, who you are, and what you have learned. Remember, Jesus Christ will always lead and guide you into righteousness. Depend upon him.

Tear Stained Pillow

Proverbs 12:5; 2 Corinthians 10:5, 2 Timothy 1:7; Titus 2:6; 2 Kings 20

Tear stains on my pillow, it is the place where Jesus and I met. I laid there, my eyes closed, feeling the warmth of salted tears gently making a puddle on my soft pillow. No one knows my heart and they cannot understand my purpose or struggles. The world it does not care and of course it never did. So, I laid there letting thousands of thoughts fill every corner of my mind, flooding it until I can no longer think clearly. Still, I laid there; as my soul desired to be in the presence of God. To speak and share my true feelings and deepest secrets. Although he knows my deepest emotions; I need the confirmation that he has not forgotten about me. I am pushed aside and left alone with a tear stained pillow.

My tears speak for me. They correlate with my moans and groans which he discerns. There is a facet of thoughts and emotions; something only God recognizes because he is the designer. If anything falls apart, he can put it together. Pity is the host of this party and Humor has not arrived. It is not well known but Jesus bottles the tears, showers rain, and gives sunshine. He never complaints, but, listens and comforts. It is neither a song nor distress signal it is a time to think on the glorious works of art painted by Jesus Christ.

He is the keeper of my mind, the council of all righteousness. He cast out images of hatred and deceit. Bringing into captivity every thought that does not exemplify him. As I lay my cluttered and confused head on my tear stained pillow, Jesus provide sanity and peace when Faith seems so far away. He is the discerner of my thoughts, erasing guilt, my tears are the witness of my struggles and reflections of troubling things. Jesus knows the ingredients that causes tears to form a stream that moves at a pace depending on what are the normality's or natures of it. Tear drops is the representation of how a person feels and they know why tears exist.

The Lord knows, sees, and hears the cries from his people. Truly he is full of compassion to heal and deliver those with a desire; to be free from the grips of sin. It is nothing to impossible for the Lord our God; for he is the same and changes not. Although tears become our meat, we must desire to walk by the righteous principles and serve with an upright heart. Faith, Trust, Confidence, and Salvation determines our relationship. Tear stained pillows are limited editions. Learn to build stronger communications with Jesus Christ, bring forth a humble heart, and He will dry your tear stained pillow, with joy.

Unsung Failures
Isaiah 59

Unsung failures not known, never heard of, not praised, and celebrated. Throughout life disappointments, all have sinned and some still desire the pleasures of the flesh. These are self-regulations at inappropriate standards that have hindered relationships with the Lord as well as with others. There is a tendency to blame the abundance of these unsung failures on society, parents, and friends, but we have yet to blame ourselves.

As believers of a Living God we need to not only understand but identify those unsung failures and present them to the Lord in the form of repentance. Our offenses are many in the sight of God, they remain with us and we know them. Unsung failures are failing to recognize hidden sins and they must be brought to confession. The Lord gives us a chance to confess our sins before he uncovers them.

Unsung failures has a negative impact on our character. Still we continue to wait with patience, hoping to overcome trials and tribulations. I applaud all, for not becoming unjust to one another, but unto ourselves. We are afraid to testify of the convictions and humiliations.

Unsung failures are deceptive and an enemy to all—especially those that practice hiding and ignoring their faults. We are witnesses against ourselves. So much time is given to covering sin, and less time is given to professing, which damages and hurts your growth in Jesus Christ.

The unsung are not honored to celebrate as in song or story. They are hidden talents and thoughts. Good deeds are not motivated by man, and distress crushes and oppresses. Go before The LORD and make known your case. Discuss your faults and explain them from the heart. With great sincerity, he washes and purges away the impurities hindering growth in Him. Oppression tugs at the mind, invading whatever peace you have found. What strong expectations can result from unsung failures? Nothing simply blurred visions.

The Soul Knows Right Well
Psalms 139; Ecclesiastes 12

Jesus is the Master of the most secretive thoughts, whether good or bad. He knows our doings before they are done and the prime intentions if there are any. Whatever is in the inner part of the soul, it cannot be hidden from him. He speaks life where there is none to be found. When the heart is broken in bits and pieces, he is there waiting to mend it back together. It is not Christ that breaks the relationship. Not at all, he is ready to reveal what is damaged and the areas that are torn down. He governs our success and monitors the failures.

If angry, take not counsel from the wicked, because their opinion will invade your mind. There are many questions and few answers to explain their devious ways. The lies are cutting edge and imprisons the heart of the most vulnerable Child of God. Daily it appears as if the wickedness consumes victory. Where is the justice for the remnant standing and waiting for the derision to fade in thin air?

We cannot find joy for a second. Life teaches on the complexity of different struggles. Life is its first name and burdens it is second. None can be trusted that resides within; not even one. Its hypocritical disguise hunts the pure in heart. To eliminate righteousness and encourage a thirst for rebelliousness. How can a broken heart contain positive thoughts? They cannot take control of their mind because it has wandered from distractions and loses train of thoughts. All mirroring the deceitful trails of oppression and illusions that become as real as we make them.

Never mind the struggles, praise The Lord for His wonderful acts and gift of mercy. We are fearfully and wonderfully made in his image and created to worship and exhort Jesus Christ. Our whole duty is to fear God and keep his commandments. His works are marvelous, and the soul knows right well. His mercy extends from generation to generation and it never runs low. We are fashioned in His image and trained to walk in the richness of his power and glory.

So, separate from the ailments of life turmoil and focus strongly on creating a bond with the Holy Ghost to help leap over the most towering mountain. The Soul Knows Right Well, its keeper, we are equipped to stand tall, with our feet deeply buried in the soil full of the rich minerals of mercy, grace, glory, and the honor of Jesus Christ Our Lord and Savior.

His Covenant
Psalm 89:37 Psalm 89:2; Proverbs 8; Proverbs 11

Jesus Christ, His covenant is everlasting, and his Word is sure. He is not a man, that he should lie; neither the son of man, that he should repent. If he said it, will he not do it? or has he spoken, and will he not make it good? The Lord is faithful to all generations and we have heard the testimonies of how he has delivered or showed up in the nick of time, when someone wanted to give up. These testimonies speak of the trust placed within the hands of the living God. His trust is known throughout the land and taught from generation to generation.

The Church make room for the congregation to testify during Testimony service as part of God's faithfulness to them who serve and trust in his authority. Through experience, the witness knew Jesus Christ would perform all things spoken and revealed by him. Every human being has a testimony of His unconditional love as a covenant keeper. He allows us to wake up to a world filled with the view of the ocean, sun, and to feel the blowing of the wind against the skin.

The unwise go in the way of their understanding. Many believe mankind has created all things seen. Without counsel the people fall; perishing because of lack of knowledge; man cannot control the gravity or the boundaries of the sea. Jesus Christ gave the sea the decree that the waters should not pass his commandment when he appointed the foundation of the earth.

Ignorance promotes carnal thinking, there is always a break down, flaw, or mishap. None of these failures or disappointments are found in Our LORD and Savior Jesus Christ. Not only is he a trustworthy covenant keeper, but he is also a perfectionist. If designed by him, it will work and serve its purpose. Everything governed is created by his hand, and the good works He wrought are flawless, and perfect.

Often we appear confused, and complexed. Regardless of the relationship with Jesus Christ, he hates sin for its stinks in his nostrils. He can deliver and destroy. For the sake of his name, Christ will continue to show us mercy and grace. On many occasions, we have cast him aside for wickedness and lustful desires. Without grudges, He takes us back and washes away all our sins.

Faith and Hope
Hebrews 11:1; Luke 17:5; 2 Thessalian 3:2;
Romans 4:17; Hebrews 11:1-12
Romans 15:4; Romans 5:5

When a broken vessel askes forgiveness, The LORD embraces them and does not turn away. His mercy and grace is eternal and is forever establish in the heavens, Although, many may find this hard to believe; what is spoken and written will come to pass. He remains faithful to every word spoken by the prophet and written upon scrolls. As believers, we learned the harshness of life experiences; but later was taught how to be victorious in the Holy Ghost. Life can't train; if given the opportunity, it will introduce damaging blows to shake, crush, or destroy your foundation. For these reasons, the Holy Spirit teaches us endurance and the power in standing in the fullness of your faith in Jesus Christ. When we begin to believe and trust in the Lord, in return, his anointing helps to increase our hope.

The Holy Ghost reminds all that Faith is the substance of things hoped for the evidence of things not seen. Hope makes not a shame; because of the love of God which is shed abroad in our hearts by the Holy Ghost. It is an act of dedication by placing trust and confidence in the hand of Jesus. Believing in his word and trusting that he can perform both what is written and spoken. It's more of an assurance that without doubt, you believe in what cannot be seen. But, your faith relies in Jesus Christ.

The doctrine of Jesus Christ is filled with riches and supports your eagerness to know him in fullness. How can any believe unless they exemplify their belief through faith? Truly the Lord works in ways unknown, but none can recognize his words unless they have studied its purpose. Sometimes, desperation clutters the mind and clogs the ears, because of the faintness of heart.

Humanity adopts disbelief making it a negative habit. We have grown accustomed to hearing the failing factors associated with it as others downplay our abilities to succeed. Many seek proof of an action or thing before believing. As Saints, we should imitate a band of cheerleaders and come on one accord exalting Jesus Christ for the glorious works he has done. Worship acknowledges His power and majesty as Lord and Savior. The Lord chose to navigate our confirmation through spoken oracles, reading his word, or by using simple lyrics to a song. Similar to cheerleaders, praising their favorite team, we should adopt the Spirit of worship and praise to show our investment and dependency upon Him.

Not only does the word of God gives light; it also nourishes the soul. The constitution of the gospel is given as added support to provide clarity. Believing is his ability to deliver, and set free must takes root in the heart, and then it will reflect in our lives. Have faith and confidence in trust and acknowledging that the Lord can do what you desire. Through faith, we understand the greatness of our expectations, and Jesus will perform his promises as written. No form of persuasion is needed with our hearts, which we solely believe that he come through each time.

By faith, our petitions are fulfilled, and the substance of reality contends with us the action is not seen; but expected. Thus, we expect the greatness of his anointing, glory, and honor. Spiritually many eyes cannot see clearly to attain the resolution of the circumstance or situations. It is suitable for the soul to believe that Christ will deliver, and reward based on our faith.

There are reasons to hope! Whatever was written before time is for our learning. So, we endure hardships without further excuse. Why should we wrestle with the difficulties and uncertainties? Do not allow corruptible thinking to darken the heart and be not ashamed of the gospel. Impenitent hearts are far from dignity and obedience. Out of much affliction and anguish, we cry for unknown reasons, so we are swallowed up with pain. Be not ashamed of past experiences for tribulations teaches patience, and patience gave experience, and from experience, many have gained hope. Hope in Jesus Christ makes us not ashamed because as Saints, we know without a doubt that the love of God is shed abroad within our hearts.

=Whatever, we must endure, it is performed with patients. Often, we are confronted with trials that we must go through, without a choice. If many of us could choose a trial free life, without further thinking, we would pursue the fantasy. Life-changing experiences build hope; no one else can deliver you from the fire but Jesus himself. When we have achieved such patience, the trial becomes a testimony to share with another. Tribulation increases our faith in the Sovereignty of God. The experience of hope is a set up towards experiencing God, and through him, we may gradually increase in the knowledge obtained from the Holy Ghost. Christ has spoken and will confirm all things promised; genuinely, he is not a God of deception nor deceit.

Why Are You Tripping

Acts of Deception
Colossians 2

All the time! Someone or something will try to deceive you. Stand on what you believe is right and honorable to yourself and towards others. Do not entertain acts of deception or the thought of it. Yes, the Lord has foreknowledge of all things. Yet we are to delight ourselves in seeking what is of the Spirit and not of the flesh. Concentrate on how you can please God and do not fall into deception. Instead, avoid temptation and the need to indulge in wrongful and selfish acts presented as sweet candy.

If bitten a little, its taste might be pleasant and desirous. Avoid curiosity; you do not have to know anything outside of holiness. (Touch not; taste not; handle not; Which all are to perish with the using;) after the commandments and doctrines of men?

Remember the old cliché curiosity killed the cat! Following matters of the heart can lead to a path of destruction. Traveling the wrong path will lead you into transgression and a life full of sin. People will love to see you fall into acts of deception and then laugh at your filthy garments. You have the power and authority to overcome all things, which does not align with the principles of righteousness. Stay with Jesus Christ, and cleave to the Holy Ghost, which is profitable for your soul.

Learning Obedience
1 Corinthians 13; Deuteronomy 32; Joshua 1; 1 Samuel 15

After becoming a believer in Jesus Christ many learned habits were dismissed. Freely, open your mind and soul to the Biblical principles and Gospel of Truth. Agreeing to accept and understand old habits are not associated with the Spirit of God. During the stages of childhood, we behaved as a child having no understanding of the mysteries of God. Traditional values confused our sense, and common knowledge elevated to worldly wisdom. As we matured in the knowledge of Christ, we put away childish things. Common knowledge disintegrated and the Holy Ghost transformed and ripened our sense of instruction to follow righteousness.

Learning obedience takes persistence and total devotion. In such an extraordinary way as the Word of God begins to manifest and old secular thoughts are relinquished and replaced with the Wisdom of God. We know His Word and listens in a state of submission. We are imitating Jesus Christ in holiness and humility by turning to search for him and desiring to be in His presence. We are his people and he is our God; therefore, we know to do his statues and judgments so that we can keep and do them with all our heart and soul. Meditating on his word day and night and learning to observe to do according to all that is written. The word of the Lord will make our way prosperous and give us good success because to obey is better than any sacrifice that we can offer to Him.

Your Life Story

If you had an eraser, how would you rewrite your life story? Would you erase all the values learned from your parents? From a child, our parents outlined our foundation to follow their norms and values by embedding their sinful thoughts and actions in our hearts. Some of their mistakes seemed justified because, possibly, they were misled as well. So, here we are at a place in time thinking about the next move. One day, we realized the point of correction began in Jesus Christ, author and finisher of our faith. How can anyone erase years of corrupt learning and useless secular practices?

When you became a follower of Jesus Christ, many things were changed and shifted around. He cleansed your heart from all unrighteousness and placed you on a new path to travel. To succeed, you must be willing to open your mind and soul to new rules and regulations which dictate Christianity. Moreover, accept and understand the facts to be truthful; because somethings are no longer acceptable to who or what you are trying to do and become. For example, when your parents continuously told you to keep up with your things and or not to take off your pieces of clothing or take care of your belonging. The instructions were teachable moments, and the items possibly were irreplaceable. Honestly, you did not always obey their commands. As you got older, you begin to acknowledge your strengths physically, emotionally, and spiritually. Later you realized the importance of those instructions or "grown-up rules." They were set in place to give you a sense of safety and responsibility. Memories that you now look back on and laugh.

How do you erase the norms of past psychological thinking? Repentance cleanses and helps to reframe our hearts to accept salvation and its spiritual things? For years we stored up every acceptable value, just to create a personalized character. Now, your thoughts are just that— "your thoughts." Your emotions, it's just that—"your emotions," of what you feel about situations or circumstances. Much time is spent pleasing a dying world that no one knows exist. Every day someone hopes to be accepted by others. Now, you have awakened from a lost state of unconsciousness. You are willing to refocus on what is meaningful and pleasing to a loving God. Still, the question remains; "how would you rewrite your life story?" Can you replace the characteristics attached to your personality? Can you convert your mind as you continue struggling to erase a lifetime of sinful traits, having profited nothing positive? We must learn obedience, for this is pleasing to Jesus Christ. Learn to be taught by the Holy Ghost.

This Is Your Song
Deuteronomy 31

When The Lord brings us into our possessions, all are joyous and full of excitement. After he has blessed His people, they turn from serving him to follow other gods.

Peradventure: by chance or uncertainty?
It could be, maybe, possibly!
Perhaps, to think or interfere with having certainty as reliable evidence.
Or could it be something as being possible?
Or could it be defined?
Is it by what we believe to be impossible?
You may pick and choose!

All things are possible with Jesus Christ.

Peradventure, when God gives you a song, it plays within your heart, beating in conjunction with the rhythms of happiness.

A smile slowly emerges as tears joyously flow. We think of the tender mercies and the ability of God to work out the situation. The tears of dependence describe the abundance of faith placed in him. As an invisible God, He enlightens our eyes to envision his mighty acts disbursed upon those that are called by his name. Touched by the Spirit, through worship and praise, we call upon his name. Our heart lift its voice and replies, 'this is our song," he has given a new melody to comfort our souls. It is soothing, bringing peace when none can be found.

Hey, this is your song and testimony. Encourage yourself in the Lord to stand when it feels like you are falling. He is the keeper of all who seeks to know and find Him. In the book of the Law it is written, and many has spoken of His many promises to the faithful. They are love letters that never get old, true, and the ink never stains. The struggles and victories create the melodies which replays amid difficult times of uncertainty. Hey, it is your song and you can rewrite it as you please. But the lyrics written by the finger of God will never change. It has a beat of its own; every soul can learn its beat, study the chords, and defeat the enemy. It is your choice to stand still or move. I am convinced, His Word declares happiness to those clinging to their faith. There are quite a few lyrics in the Biblical book of Knowledge and Truth. Go ahead flip the pages and receive the visible tokens of his presence. Hope with a greater expectation, He can and will nurture your existence with soft harmonies which were eloquently written to serenade the body and soul.

The Word Is An Instrument
John 1:14; Romans 3; Isaiah 55:11

The word is an instrument of encouragement to the soul. It alters a confused mind and calms a troubled heart. The Lord Jesus takes great care with keeping all things spoken and written by him. He sets them as milestones established with older generations, embraced by the young, and he is a magnificent creator of humanity. No one or nothing has the ability or the power to strike his authority from the four corners of the world.

Many have walked carefully in his presence; but, no one can walk in his place; neither endure such pains in suffering as he. The Father chose and gave his Son, Jesus Christ to become a propitiation through faith in his blood, to declare his righteousness for the remission of past sins, through the forbearance of God. He is "The Word," which was made flesh and lived among us. Jesus Christ is the Master and Savior to all who believe in Him. Humanity is fragile, weak vessels, easily persuaded, and always afraid.

The Lord is a God of Battles, walking before his people. Be strong and courageous because The Lord would never fail. Continue to go forth and inherit the gifts of the Holy Ghost. Find a sacred place to read the book of the law. Learn to hear and fear the Lord and do all the words he commanded. The Word is a powerful instrument. It speaks of the divine presence and appearances of Jesus Christ. He gives us future revelations of things not seen and the good things to come. Trouble befalls the hearts of them who forsake and break the covenant vowed unto him.

As a result of their disbelief, they become afraid of rising storms and raging winds. The Lord is dedicated to the strength of the people. He is walking before them, leading the way in such simplicity that would build faith and hope. Some believers have genuinely fell short in trusting in the everlasting hands of God. Their issues of warring and tribulation have weakened their foundation in Christ. So, they are sought out as prey for the enemy without a place to hide. They are no longer anchored in the precepts of wisdom, sadly forgetting that God never fails. There are many benefits of the law. Jesus knows who is calling on his name.

He sees the hypocrites and hears his people. The Word of God is an instrument sent forth out of His mouth: it will not return unto Him void, but it will accomplish that which He please, and it will prosper in the thing whereto he sent it.

Take Heed and Know Who You Are

Control Your Thoughts
Romans 8; James 1:19

People find ways to disturb your peace of mind and to agitate your last nerve. The more you think about it, they do it regularly, and emotionally you feel powerless. You see, many Christians allow others to walk over them and refuse to speak up. So, the affliction weighs heavy on the heart and perplexes the mind. In your dreams, you have beat the person until you were satisfied and victorious. No one saw you win or saw the agitator defeated. It is funny, but you know it is true.

If you ever watched the Spider-Man cartoons, when danger was near, he would say, "My Spider Senses are starting to tingle," or something of the sort. Then, he would change into his superhero costume to save the day. He was attentive to the dangers and acted accordingly. Cool analogy, huh? We can learn a lot from watching cartoons; no one is too old to laugh.

In comparison, allow your spiritual senses to alert you of the dangers that are near. The Holy Ghost helps us to identify the threats attacking your heart and mind. Swiftly, he uses the Word of God as a defense to retaliate against carnal thoughts.

As anger flares, the Holy Ghost showers the heart with wisdom, knowledge, and understanding. Spiritual thoughts such as, to be swift to hear, slow to speak, s and slow to wrath. Because the wrath of man works not the righteousness of God. Do not act on impulse; take time to think before acting. Our response should be of righteousness and to behave otherwise is not of God.

People know exactly what to say to intimidate God's people. When we get angry, it brings embarrassment, shame, and depression. To protect against wickedness, remember the teachings received. Then, the Holy Ghost knows how to interpret the ignorance of others. Anger, embarrassment, shame, and depression are ungodly tactics to confiscate our peace and cloud our better judgment in handling situations.

Physically, you feel embarrassed, ashamed, and wondering if you were a coward in letting them belittle your character. These thoughts impact your self-esteem, and depression comes to sit directly in your lap without comfort. Allow the Holy Ghost to communicate what is right and profitable to your soul. It will bring firepower to diminish unpleasant thoughts. What you do not want is to act out. Instead, bring every unpleasant thought under subjection to the Laws of God. Children of God should practice walking after the Spirit and do things of the Spirit. If you walk in the flesh, the carnality of your mind will deceive and win.

Take a moment to think about what is taking place in your heart and mind spiritually. The adversary uses flesh against the flesh to distract and destroy the Children of God. If we are not careful, we can find ourselves losing and enemy winning. Sometimes, we have to step back and evaluate the entire picture. Look at the details, the colors, the shapes, and allow the Spirit of Discernment given by the Holy Ghost to decipher the problem.

No, Not One!

God will leave his people for a while, just to test their faith.
There is quietness, no turmoil, neither echoes in the wind.
Closing your eyes, try hard to hear the voice of God.
The outpouring of your soul desires to hear
a word, but there is nothing.
In your visions of the night, you dream upon
the presence of Jesus Christ.
You learn He can do whatever he pleases.
Who is going to say that he is an unjust God? No, not one.
In all his righteousness, he gives his people April showers.
Showers of love reflects the multitude of his tender mercies.
Who can say that he has broken his promises? No, not one.
For he has been a covenant keeper from the beginning.
He never forgets and always remembers
those who walk upright in heart.
Who can dare to speak and accuse him of selfish deeds? No, not one.
Truly, he has given and shared hidden treasures, prosperity,
and the richness of all his glory with those that are called by his name.
Who can speak such awful things about him?
No, not one. He has shown the awesomeness of his character
and identify with those declaring to know of him.
For he continuously reveals his wonderful works.
Who dares to say he is not God? No, not one.
He is a God of today, the hope of tomorrow,
the living and everlasting God.
He never falters in his doings, neither faint along the way.
He continues to uphold his purpose and commands every day.
He controls what is seen and unseen.
Who can say He has failed?
No, not one! No, not one!

Pursue
1 Samuel 30:1-21; 1 Corinthians 13:11

Acknowledge the Lord in everything pursue after what you desire from the Lord. Pursue and take back what belongs to you. Pursue after your enemy and bind him up. Pursue your enemy and stay with Jesus, and you will recover everything you lost. As we mature, we must understand there are responsibilities and obligations to follow. As we begin to mature in the gospel, there are responsibilities and obligations given to modify our behavior.

Take heed to the teachings of scripture, consider the various scriptures which provide revelations or affirmations. Enlighten the mind as we attempt to understand our responsibility to the body of Christ. Those who are within the body of Christ must have holiness, which is the very fabric of the gospel. And many other biblical writings to include separation and obedience are both deeply carved in the structure of the gospel as time passes, embrace your salvation, and pursue Jesus Christ in all things.

Beauty and Bands
Zachariah 10:1; 11:7,10,14; 13:9; Malachi 1:6

How can your soul abhor the Lord? The Creator of humanity; He that has laid the foundation of the earth and gave the spirit of man life so that he may breathe. Whom is it that dares to trespass against the Lord? Lord pour upon your people the spirit of grace and supplication. Sin and uncleanliness require an outpouring of His living waters.

Use prayer to commune with God for rain in due season. Difficult days need the latter rain to revive the abundance and richness of his mercy. The coming of the rain provides nourishment for the earth and signifies His blessings. Ask the LORD for rain; he can shower down an outpouring of the Holy Ghost to revive those hungering and thirsting for His Presence. He will enlighten the day, providing clear instructions to nurture the hearts of everyone.

Seasonal rains are the blessings poured out in its proper time. Its band stretches from the north, south, east, and west, granting seasonal mercies as a token of God's grace and favor. Beauty and Bands fall upon the just and the unjust. Likewise, his Salvation is offered and given to all who desire to serve and obey His Commandments. The Gospel is to all, and it appears in power and in the Holy Ghost. Jesus Christ died on the Cross for all to be reconciled back to His Father.

If you confess that the Lord is your Father, then where is the honor due to Him? If you confess that he is your Master, then where is his fear? We give so much credit to flesh and blood, but refuse to acknowledge the character of God. Servants cautiously obey those whom they serve as they work in obedience and respect. Somehow, we seem to have stumbled at the promise. We serve with such anger showing no honor or fear of God.

So we feast on polluted bread, which is contaminating by rebellious acts and stony hearts. Who can speak knowledge and stand in the beauty of holiness and give Jesus Christ the admiration He deserves? Pour out your heart before him with tears.

Amid the trials and tribulation, Jesus continued to give them wise instruction and sound doctrine. His love and promises would not allow him to forsake the people called by His name. Their iniquities affected the relationship with Jesus Christ, and many fell by the side and was given over to sin. The world persecuted them all day long and accounted them as sheep for the slaughter. Many wandered away from the Shepherd, straying far from Him. As a result, the LORD hid his face from the shame and allowed them to fall into captivity. They continued disobedience and dismantled the foundation built in Jesus Christ.

The Lord desired to break His covenant, which He had made with His people. Their disobedience angered Him. However, The Word of God continued to go forth, and his messengers continued preaching repentance and healing the hearts of many. The faithful few that continuously attend to the Biblical principles and upholds the commandments of God are the poor in Spirit and those who have apprehended the scriptures. To offer Salvation by the Holy Ghost, he gave Pastors to lead his sheep back to Him. The grace of Jesus Christ saves their souls and enjoins them back into a relationship with Him. The House of God is the temple that holds the beauty of holiness. In the temple, His people can worship and lift him up to celebrate a life of sanctification and holiness.

Then, Jesus Christ thought about the Bands, that He might break the unity and weaken His people to become a prey to the enemy. They continue to disobey the commandments written and breaking the covenant and relationship with the God of Salvation. These Bands stretched forth around the world.

Do not put yourself in a position to provoke God to anger. Walk upright before him and open your heart to receive The Word of God and build a relationship to guide you through the storm and rain. Unchurched folk is those that attend Church every Sunday and still refuses to grow and take the next step in the vocation in which they are called. He that has an ear, let him hear what the Spirit says unto the churches.

Red Flags
Psalm 139:23-24; Proverbs 16; Proverbs 20; Roman 7; 2 Corinthians 4; Psalm 35 Psalm 73; Psalm 103; Hebrews 2

Let the Word of God pierce to the asunder of the soul. Uproot bad habits and cling to what is good. The time has come that we must seek out ways to dig deeper in the Gospel of Jesus Christ. The prophet Jeremiah invited God's people to break up the fallow ground. Break up everything hindering your walk with the Lord. Breakaway from circumstances and situations. These things come about to test or choke the life of holiness from the inward man. Our spirit-man is the candle of the Lord and it searches the inward parts of the belly. Its integrity is created to mirror the ordinances of God. As we draw nearer to Him, he gives us the understanding; it is because of Him we live. So, the spirit-man searches the inward parts of the belly for the contents of the heart, whether it is good or wicked. From the depths of the belly, we send forth an echo and aroma of praise to symbolize our appreciation for Salvation.

Jesus Christ continues to pour out an abundance of mercy and grace, which cannot be measured by us. He chose a peculiar set of people that he wanted to offer a chance at the good things stored up in heaven. The Holy Ghost ensures grace is sufficient as it works in overtime to save miserable ungrateful souls. There is work to be done and we must strive to sharpen our knowledge and understanding of who we are in the body of Christ.

We get tired and weary of well-doing. Feelings of fatigue causes us to hallucinate and confusion affects our better judgment. In Church we look around and see the hypocrites who faithfully attend Church Service as heavy logs sitting as distractions. Their agenda is to quench the presence of the Holy Ghost. No one else desires to work, so you look around tired and burned out still trying to bare the roles of many. But, for the cause of the love of God, you faint not. Our body, the outward man or outer appearance changes as the heart matures in the knowledge of God. We suffer with Christ by crucifying the flesh daily and yielding to the Spirit of Righteousness.

When we see others struggling to serve The LORD, there is not much to do; but intercede on their behalf. Whatever might be the reason, their vision is darkened and obscured. Their refusal to praise God, blocks their deliverance from whatever is holding their hearts hostage. Clashing with the Holy Ghost is a losing battle; because it is hard to kick up against the prick. The Lord sends warnings before destruction.

The red flags are waved and ignored. Layers of disappointments, anger, and other emotions has caused their hearts to suffer. Pride and a haughty spirit are the roots of their destruction. As a result, the outer appearance remains unchanged because of their stony heart. The LORD has provided instructions to edify the House of God. However, many hearts have waxed cold and refuse to let Him in; thus, their stony hearts remain unscathed.

The Lord can rescue our souls from destruction. Howbeit, we always set ourselves up in slippery situations without understanding the hidden consequences. A sincere heart will acknowledge their mistakes, repent, and Jesus will catch them before they hit the ground. Jesus Christ is always ready to redeem the lives of His people, who he crowns with lovingkindness and tender mercies. As a result, we do not give up garnishing strength and courage from the Holy Ghost. The red flags alerts God's people of the dangers that lie ahead. He sends warnings before destruction and we should take heed of the Gospel; to maintain our FAITH.

From the abundance of the heart, we try to see the good in people who labor in the gospel with us. Amid the arrogance, we pick up the slack and let them live with the consequences of guilt and shame. We want the Glory of God to reflect on the outside so others can see the pureness of our hearts. So, the inward man is renewed day by day because of the fear of the LORD which reigns in our life.

There comes a time when we must stop and look at the situation surrounding us. We must come to the realization; we do not have the power to rescue every person in the House of God. Spiritually, they are draining the anointing of God from us, leaving our soul tired and weary. Wake up; sometimes, we must leave them hanging and blowing in the wind. One day, they will learn to anchor themselves in the Word of God and secure a stronger foundation in Him. Prayer is the most powerful tool we have in our Church toolbox. Intercede and stand in the gap for the Children of God. They must be willing to change for the edification of their salvation or Spiritually die. The red flags are waving, but they must seek God and he will send the Holy Ghost to correct their vision. Sin is a burden and it will send life in a downward spiral. In vain, they look for peace when there is none because of the conformities and the rejection of the commandments of God.

Yes, we falter in our walk with Jesus Christ. However, knowing to repent and not ignore your flaws is a big difference. Acknowledgment is to say, "yes, Lord, I have sinned before thee. I pray Lord, that you forgive me and allow me to walk before you in the Spirit of Holiness." Expect greatness from Jesus Christ and he will blow your mind each step of the way. Our epic failures are based on our actions. Will we continue to ignore the red flags or take heed to the warning signs? It is time to be more in tuned and concerned with your relationship with the Father, Son, and Holy Ghost. If your ways are pleasing unto Him, Jesus Christ will give you the desires of your heart.

Get back on track, delight yourself in the law of God after the inward man. Do not let your conscience be your guide. Because of the crooked ways chosen, your carnal thinking will bring you to shame. Allow the Holy Ghost to use the Spirit of Discernment to distinguish the good things of God and He will direct your path.

Longevity In Life
1 King 3:14; Job 5:26; Psalm 91:16; Proverbs 10:27; Matthew 7; Luke 11; Psalm 16; Job 7; Psalm 25

Everyone wants to find favor with God and wondering if he is well pleased with their life. Give the LORD a sacrificial offering which includes spending time with Him. Read the Bible, get in His presence, and worship. Walk before The LORD in truth, and in righteousness, and in uprightness of heart and he will keep you in great kindness. Seek from Jesus Christ an understanding heart to discern between good and bad. Dwell in the presence of God, a secret place, and find refuge to clear the heart and mind. Share with him what is in your heart and serenade Him in devotion with shouts of joy, hand-clapping, musical instruments, singing, lifting your hands, dancing before him, and etcetera. Spiritually, Physically, and Emotionally, create positive ways to gain long life.

Sometimes we get so caught off guard with different situations that sidetracks our thinking; we forget about The Lord. Stressful situations build up tension and works on the heart and weighs down the body. Let go and allow God to develop your integrity and uprightness, while you wait for the manifestation of the Holy Ghost.

For the defense of gospel and with much boldness abide in the Spirit of God with confidence. Continue with Him for the furtherance of your joy and FAITH. Jesus Christ is a preserver of man grants life, favour and his presence preserves our spirit. Receiving God's stamp of approval is better than the disputes argued by man. We should prefer the "blessings from God," because he awards them who diligently seeks for Him. If the wicked know how to give good gifts to their children, how much more will Jesus Christ which are in heaven give good things to them that ask him. So, ask for the gifts of God.

Get closer to God, build a life centered around His principles and apply them accordingly in all areas of your life. Prayer is the key and understanding its weight will further the trust and relationship with Christ. Learn and gain wealth of knowledge which separates you from all others because it shows you have spent a great deal of time in the presence of God. Like Moses, the skin of his face shone and people were afraid to approach him. When so much time is spent with God, a change will take place. People will be afraid to approach because the Holy Ghost will reveal their truths.

Personally, I desire God in the fullness and not come short of His Glory. Everyday, I depend on the Holy Ghost to show me the path of life because God's Presence is the fullness of my joy. The LORD IS MY EVERYTHING, HE IS THE AIR THAT I BREATHE AND I KNOW THAT THERE IS NOTHING I CAN DO WITHOUT HIM. So, I cling to Him for life and outside of Him nothing in this world matters; not even my children. As for me, I believe the only true love is "THE LOVE OF GOD." He will never betray or leave you alone. At his right hand there are pleasures forevermore. Learn to prefer the grace of God. He will preserve you in all His ways. In his hand is long life and to receive it, we must walk in His ways, keep his statutes and commandments, and then He will lengthen our days. Jesus Christ, Son of the Living God, is a keeper and will preserve His people from this generation and forevermore.

Lovingkindness

Jeremiah 31; John 3; 1John 4; Psalm 103;
Lamentations 3; Ephesians 2; Titus 3 Deuteronomy
7; Psalm 36; 2 Thessalonians 3; 2 Timothy 2

It is True! The Lord Loves You. His love and kindness has drawn you into his covenant promises and took communion with you. The Lord's love is magnified in the giving of his son Jesus Christ to reconcile humanity back to him. For the sole purpose of redemption and salvation, Jesus Christ was given as a propitiation for a sacrifice. He has commanded his love; it is our duty to believe in him receive life and not perish.

He that loves not knows not God; for God is love, this is his Spirit and essence. His love was manifested and spread abroad. He sent his only son into the world to offer life and salvation. It was not because we loved Him; first, he loved us, feeble and rebellious souls. Yet, we crucify Him daily with our stubbornness and inability to love him more. His everlasting Mercy is from everlasting to everlasting. Upon them, who fear or obey him, his righteousness extends for generations and is never-ending.

Every morning his mercy is renewed; his faithfulness is great! It was by his mercy that he saved us when he blotted out all our sins. Then, Jesus Christ restored and made us whole in Him. A new growth took place, for he cut away the old branches which bare not the Fruit of the Spirit. Renewing the soul as the Holy Ghost brought newness of life. Know this, the Lord is God, and He is faithful. Obedience to his commandments gives mercy to all who love and obey Him to a thousand generations. The perfection of his mercy reigns in heaven, and with great patience are his sheep protected. His lovingkindness is before our eyes: and we must walk in the Gospel of Truth.

Inherited Spiritual Weaknesses
Hebrews 10; Leviticus 10;

Spiritual Weaknesses are infirmities of the flesh. They lie isolated and are profoundly in our thoughts, waiting for the perfect time to surface. Inherited weaknesses are long-standing propensities transformed into strongholds and have taken residents in our lives. These weaknesses were passed down as generational curses that refuse to let go. So, they sit like lonely islands waiting to occupy the next vessel.

Inherited spiritual weakness were prevelant in the years of bondage and poorness in spirit. The moanings of oppression and depression trickle from the repetitiveness of speech. Rise from the bareness of nothings and stand firm in the fear and admiration of the Holy Ghost. The LORD is the same God that never grows old.

Change the setting and conform to the pearls of wisdom that dangling high from Heaven's door. Reach up, grab hold of your integrity, and build a foundation with Jesus Christ as the cornerstone. Bind up generational curses and reset your family values. It is never too late! Stand tall like the trees in Lebanon and claim the strength that lies within the arm of Jesus Christ.

Inherited Spiritual Weaknessess takes residence in the heart of the weakest sheep. Reclaim your joy for happy are the people of God because they were saved by Him. He is your help and the sword of excellency! Let your voice ring throughout the land. The LORD has given us the power to tread over the enemy: and nothing shall by any means hurt you.

Hold your head upward and look to the God of your Salvation, rid yourself of the bareness of speech having no meaning. Rehearse in the ear of God, the desires of your heart. Cling to every biblical promise spoken before the foundation of the world. Jesus Christ is the antidote for every problem, and his "blood" erases the stains.

New generations are coming, and the genealogy of your family will continue to grow. The new babies and our children are birth into this world innocent and without blemishes. We must teach them all the statutes which the LORD has spoken, using the blood as a covering to their hearts and souls. So they may know to wear their amour, use the bow, and the Sword of the Spirit to war against the enemy.

Inherited spiritual weaknesses are wasted beliefs and can be reversed by teaching our children the importance in serving Jesus Christ. We tend to think, "That is just the way I am." or "I can't help it." As a result, we don't think about changing, and if so, it seems impossible. Human standards of strength and weakness are overturned by God's perspective and may be used for his glory. These weaknesses will never go unnoticed by Jesus Christ and soon will be uprooted from its nucleus.

What happens...

What happens to the years of growth when you thought that you had it all together? When it appeared that you were giving everything in your soul. Trying to elevate others into the realm of holiness; so, that they too could experience the presence of God. In your heart, there is so much spiritual excitement that you wish it would pour upon the heart of the congregation. Hoping, if you push a little harder to lift them, all would desire to feel the blast of the breath of his nostrils; and showing how it would graciously blow away every plaguing issue.

What happens when you are at the height of praise, leading, and introducing God's people to the majestic powers of happiness and the joy his presence would bring when we are on one accord? Clothing wet from perspiration, eyes fluttering with tears, your knees are weak under the presence of the Holy Ghost. As you open your eyes, you noticed, only a select few are interacting, and others are not. Some starring directly at you; others are sitting with arms crossed in strong anticipation that soon it will be all over.

What happens when you are putting forth your best to stand in the gap, interceding, crying, and asking God to heal a body of believers that are broken and fearful of surrendering unto Him? So many are afraid that they may lose everything if they totally gave up their secular beliefs. Suddenly, you felt that no one was praying with you.

Okay. Well...what happens when the LORD allows you to discern strife amongst believers. Many pretend to love you. Yet, they assemble to set traps, clutter your thoughts, and intimidate your assignment from God? Later, you find that they have pinned you up against the wall. Similar to an alley cat that is trapped with nowhere to run. So, you go into "Attack Mode."

What happens when all of a sudden, you lose it? On more than one occasion. Only to feel the pointed fingers poking at your heart and the ridiculing sound of laughter coming from the enemy. They are bent over oddly laughing at your calamity.

Okay. Okay. What happens when DEFEAT feels a bit heavy sitting in your lap, staring you straight in the eye and saying, "Call it quits," because it has won?

The mere feeling of aftershock invades your peace and your sleep. For, Defeat has obtained a

Devastating victory. It has channeled your secular strengths and dominated your will-power. Without a solid purpose or meaning, you begin to feel EMPTY and out of place. FRUSTRATED and EMBARRASSED that you allowed the wicked to ANGER and TRIUMPH. Now, What Will Happen!!!!

TAKE BACK YOUR WILL AND POWER TO REGROUP, TAKE THE LOVE OF GOD AND REPENT. THIS TIME GO HARDER AND STRONGER THAN EVER BEFORE.

The Problem Solver

We get so frustrated about the little things that make us so crazy.
Later in the day, everything began to settle;
we take a deep breath and exhale.
Then, our minds start to replay every little thing that happened,
and the Holy Ghost speaks to the heart and say,
"You could have handled it a lot better."

During times such as these, we never think at that specific moment,
for this reason, the Gospel of Truth reminds us, James 1:19
"Wherefore, my beloved brethren, let every man be swift to hear,
slow to speak, slow to wrath,"
Stop for a moment to listen, think about your words before you speak,
and then slowly react. Many times, we need only
a little Manna to nurture your soul.

Stop Being a Fraidy Cat

Strive for Perfection

Sometimes your day may appear a bit cloudy, and feelings of guilt may overwhelm your heart and mind. Yet, the most important thing is to remain focused on what is important to you and not the people that you see daily. Their dreams are not your dreams, and their strength is not the strength that can uphold your purpose. Get into the realm of practicing how to commune with The Living God. Entrust your thoughts to Jesus Christ, stand back and watch Him design the perfect plan just for you. Every day will not be like the previous day. Each time that you have fallen does not truly dictate your ending. It is important to fight when you don't feel like fighting and smile when you think you have lost. As Children of God, we tend to beat ourselves for each time that we have fallen short of the Glory of God. In actuality, the best practice is to walk in a "Mode of Repentance."

Never stop moving! If you fail in life, there is no one to fault but yourself. So, stand up, dust yourself off, and take a good look in the mirror. While looking at your reflection in the mirror, laugh and pat yourself on the back. Life is too short for misery to be in control, apprehending your joy, and seizing your strength. Understand the Power and Authority that reigns in your vessel. Understand that you are an heir to the Kingdom of God, a chosen generation, a royal priesthood, a holy nation, a peculiar people; that you should show forth the praises of him who has called you out of darkness into his marvelous light.

Nothing can hold you back unless you give that 'thing' or "something" power over your anointing. Practicing to become VICTORIOUS takes willpower and perseverance. As Soldiers in the Army of The LORD, Christ has no coward Soldiers. The Blood of Jesus Christ is the same, and it will never lose its power. We have become weakened by diverse trials and tribulations. Many have forgotten how to stand against the snares of adversity. Our main goal is to come out of bondage, hold fast to the promises of God, and press toward the mark for the prize of the high calling of God in Christ Jesus. Nothing should restrain your perseverance. Apply your Praise, Increase your Level of Praise, Refocus your Level of Praise and Praise

The Name of Our Lord and Saviour Jesus Christ until you have received your breakthrough.

The LORD that we serve is simple! It does not take a lot of big words to get a simple point across. Simplicity is favorable when sharing the Word of God to a dying generation. Many remain trapped in their hearts and mind, trying with every ounce of desperation to be set free. Life is beautiful because Jesus Christ gives his people a new day, every day, to get it right another day. I love The LORD, and I won't take it back; because He has been good to me.

May The LORD and Our Saviour Jesus Christ continue to shine upon you and keep you in times when you are not able to keep yourself. We must find ourselves in and between the Word of God, and walk closely behind Him. Sometimes, sit back and think of the days when the Pentecostal Church Mothers led the prayer at the Altar. Did not your soul burn with excitement and joy. Searching for the "Fire of the Holy Ghost" is fulfilling to the Soul. The Soul yearns to be embraced by the power of its anointing. You will be amazed! Jesus is still holding meetings at the Altar. No one's running to be the first-in-line. In today's world, some may believe it doesn't take all the speaking in tongues, shouting, crying, and running. Well, for some, it takes all that and a lot more. When you are searching and looking for something, you have to be persistent with your search.

It takes no effort for Jesus to be Jesus. It takes a lot of effort for us to remain Saved, Sanctified, and Holy Ghost filled. Always guard the Word of God in your heart and use your gift of discernment to recognize deceitful practices. You will be amazed! Still, follow peace with all men, and holiness, without which no man shall see the Lord.

To God Be The Glory and Honour.

Look Up, and Live, In Jesus Name!

Take A "Leap Of Faith"

Believe In Your Success!

We are giving the necessary tools and resources to reach
far beyond what others may think or express.
Your future is as bright as you make it and becomes duller
the moment you stop believing in yourself.
Do not allow the world to design an image of who you are.
On the contrary, trust that Jesus Christ will
lead you in the right direction.
He can uphold your existence, higher than the moon and stars.
Look up, reach high, and smile at the Great I Am!

Stand Up and Stand Tall

Stand up, stand tall, recognize how high you are.
Look up, go higher, reach far beyond the clouds above.
Stand up, what do you see? Way up high! You are doing it now!
If you look down, you will see just how far you have come.
Stand up, Stand tall! Did you reach Heaven's door?
Knock hard, allow Christ to hear your call.
Tarry and wait you will see, just how much He loves you and me.

He is right there; keep knocking, you will see.
Christ is there waiting to show the world how much you really believe.
Stand up, Stand Tall! Are you paying attention at all?
Did you tell Him? Did you talk?
Did you say anything at all?
It is okay, and do not worry. Encourage all to stand up and stand tall!
Christ will catch them before they fall.
Remember this: remember that Christ's Words are everlasting.
I told you this, and that—keep knocking and he will answer.
Now, that is a fact.

No One To Blame
Psalm 17

Sometimes, we find ourselves crying out to the LORD, asking that he be attentive to sound echoing from deep within. Desperations seep from the pain that trembles at the presence of fear and anguish. The righteous inquires at the hand of God, knowing that his judgment is swift and persuasive to the enemy. Pretending hearts lie and do not wage highly on The Holy Ghost.

Distinctively, they cling to their weakest efforts of deception and unpredictable torment. They are pretending to learn when they are afraid to confess their faults. So, they falter, and the shyness starts to fade. The façade they once wore is no more. God reveals their true colors, and the unveiling may be damaging. Jesus Christ gave us life to enjoy. As time progress, we will suffer a few bumps and bruises. Others may have deep wounds and scarring from traumatic incidents. Still, there is no one to blame. The person used to inflict such pain is not remorseful. Instead, they are glad to have you stuck in a dimension where you cannot move forward.

Take away the blame and ask the LORD to remove the reproach. Your petition should be, "LORD, I want to become new in you." Everything you desire to mimic, according to the Holy Ghost. People will pretend they care about your pain, struggles, or happiness. If the truth is told, they are glad when you stop whining, let go, and allow God to manifest healing. Allow the Holy Ghost to change the countenance of your face in righteousness. Stop wearing your whole life on the sleeves for all to see. Receive the awakening within your soul, and Jesus Christ will satisfy your desires and build upon the Faith and Trust placed in him.

Finding someone else to take the fall or blame for life mishaps is vanity. Their minds are joined and fashioned after fleshly instincts and do not mirror the Spiritual System of Holiness and Righteousness. If you reject healing and deliverance, your emotions shift to babbling, insensible words. Thus, you become snared by the words of your mouth. The words you speak escape from the presence of righteousness, like an insect crawling to find a deep hole to hide. Uttering words without purpose or meaning fades in the presence of Jesus Christ, for his eyes witnesses all equal things. In the presence of the Holy Spirit, pretending hearts become apprehended, conviction prevails and surrenders in obedience.

Listen! There is "no one to blame." Pick up the broken and shattered pieces of your life and pour it in the hand of God. Watch how he mends back each piece like a puzzle without the jagged edges. As you read the Word of God, The Holy Ghost will allow you to experience the pain and joy of others. Let me give an example, at my Church, every first and third Saturday, we hold an intercessory prayer for the women and young ladies. As we read the Word of God together, the Holy Ghost allows us to find ourselves in between the pages. Sometimes, we laugh, and others, we may cry. It is because the Holy Ghost brings to remembrance how Jesus Christ has helped us to overcome so many barriers. So, the tears began to flow because our hearts recognized the power of God. Now, if we did not move forward; but stalled on past issues, we would have never grown in the Word of God or experienced his goodness. The Word says, "Oh, taste and see that the LORD is good." In so many ways and more than we can imagine, Jesus Christ has been good to us.

Jesus Christ proves our hearts; he visits us in our darkest hours to bring light to desolated areas. Infirmities chisel away at your faith until you can merely stand. While hiding from the enemy, in silence, remain quiet, speak nothing, and listen for the voice of God. The LORD sends His warring angel to quiet the chaotic moments of perils and blind the enemy for the sake of His sheep. The enemy frowns at the Word of God because Power reigns with the LORD and Savior. When words are spoken from his lip, He hides His sheep deeper in his pavilion—overshadowing their presence by His Holy wings. So, as we journey along the way, his presence keeps our footsteps from slipping along the path of righteousness. There, he inclines his ear to hear the voice of his sheep. If you go stray, the enemy lay like a lion; greedy of his prey, lurking in secret places.

The LORD's presence compasses your reigns and shows loving-kindness, delivering with his right hand. Trust in him, and he will keep you as the apple of his eye, hiding you under the shadow of his wings. Hide from the enemy, search for a secure place deep inside his pavilion. When the enemy rises, the sword of righteousness will deliver your soul from those of the world. In this life, they are given their portion to devour; destroying it until nothing is left. As for you, stand up, stand tall, and obey his commandments. When the enemy is subdued, Jesus will reward according to your faith in his power and strength. There is no one to blame for our mishaps in life. His law has a shadow of good things to come; so, wait upon the LORD to renew your strength.

The Reflection of Life
2 Samuel 7; 1 Thessalonians 5;
1 Corinthians 6; 1 Corinthians 10

The Lord had given King David rest from war. He had peace and time to reflect on his current position, success, and future goals. To express his gratitude, King David desired to build a house for the Ark of God to dwell. As he reigned as king over Israel, God showed King David favor, fought battles for him, and remembered his prayers of forgiveness. He realized the greatness of God's love, glory, and honor. King David evaluated "The Reflection of Life," and realized, God has given him rest from all his enemies.

When there is peace, we have time to "reflect on life's struggles." What can you give to The Lord? Employ your thought to think about ways to indulge in the Presence of God. Once decided, settle down and revamp your life. Balance it with moments of prayer, worship, and praise. Delight yourself in the law of the LORD by meditating on it day and night. Stand in awe and offer the sacrifices of righteousness, communing with your heart while glorifying His name.

The promises we made to obey His vows, many were broken. So we try to find ways to mend back our broken relationship. After praying, searching the scriptures, repenting, and serving him, we find that there is more we would like to do. He simply requires us to obey, stand, and trust in Him.

The reflection of life is evident in our weaknesses; but, Jesus Christ gave us rest and granted peace within our walls. How often do you think about pleasing God? Are you willing to surrender your body, and how's the word of God in the heart? Now, the time has come for us to build upon the foundation of our teachings. A task that can be accomplished by surrendering everything to Him.

He has put gladness in your heart, more than in times past. The reflection of life is thought on by the wise and simple-hearted. Their worship is founded on devotion and the sweetness of the relationship with Jesus Christ. His greatness reminds us of what he has done to sustain and employ us with favor, amongst others.

The reflection of life should mimic biblical standards, which teaches us how to live. King David understood the importance of acknowledging the power of God. We are indebted to Him and whatever you do for the Kingdom of God, perform the duties for the glory of God. As we mature in our relationship with Christ, we should be mindful of the types of activities taking place within our spiritual temples.

Your body is the temple of the Holy Ghost, which is in you, which you have from God, and you are not your own. Our earthly house and this tabernacle belong to the LORD, and the very God of peace sanctifies you. God being the creator, knows how much we have polluted our house. Therefore, he has allowed us to repent, renew, and build a Tabernacle where God can rest and for the Holy Ghost.

The adversary continues to pursue God's people; He continues to deliver us. Daily, the LORD walks before us, removing stumbling blocks, keeping his flock safe from wolves, and eradicating the other nations for their safety. While walking, he spoke encouraging words and taught his people to stand in the face of fear. Yet, no one is willing or ready to build him a house to abide. After all, The LORD has accomplished in your life, are you prepared to build and give something to Jesus Christ. The reflection of life is to say, "your life does not belong to you." So, give it back to Jesus Christ. Let him command it as he pleases. Everyone owes their existence to Him.

Burden Bearer
Isaiah 1; Matthew 11; Jeremiah 3; Colossians 3

Some people are tightly wrapped in sin and searching for a way out. Suffocating from the pollution surrounding them and cannot break free. There is not a soul close enough to pry open the doors, which has shut, causing distress and anguish. A sinful nation is merely a group entangled and alienated from Jesus Christ. The backslider lifts their voice, calling the Savior by name and profess their past relationship to Him. The soul is tired and weary with the corruptive elements of the adversary. Warring in the flesh, many are sinking deeper into a bottomless pit from the weight of guilt and shame.

Rebellious acts cause them to reject building an intimate relationship with the Father. Instead of growing and becoming fruitful, so many begin to wither away from the Gospel. The love of God is faithful, and he heard their cry. The heart of the backslider returned to its first love and husbandman to forgive their iniquities. Jesus Christ is married unto the backsliding children and rescues them from a dying world to give them rest from daily care embedded in their minds. If the heart of His people would meditate and learn of His unfailing love, they can be liberated from the chain reactions of defeat past down from generational curses.

Jesus Christ knows our every weakness. Our existence depends on His strong arm to save us from our faults. He is the burden-bearer to carry us beyond our infirmities. He gives us rest from the chaotic conditions to help us build back the walls of Faith.

We have caused ourselves to war against circumstances that were out of our control by putting ourselves in tough situations revealing vulnerabilities, which the adversary uses as ammunition to destroy. Be watchful and do not be influenced by misconceptions of who you are and the God that you serve. Remain awaken in the Spirit of Holiness and do not lose focus. Avoiding or turning a deaf ear to His sayings means that you desire to abide in the flesh and not in the Spirit. As a result, you cannot comprehend and will fail to understand Jesus Christ gave the Holy Ghost to lead you out of the realm of total ignorance into the Gospel of Truth.

Indeed, Jesus Christ is a burden bearer, we must allow the Holy Ghost to manifest in our lives, and He will remove the yoke of bondage. When you slip, fall, or stumble, continue serving the LORD and with great hope, expect the best and nothing less. Never stay down and never be ashamed of your salvation. Many have fallen, refusing to get up and slips backward. Jesus has not lost one soul given to him by His Father, and his blood still cleanses and washes away the stain of sin. The word is near you; the word of God is in your mouth and your heart. Let the word of Christ dwell in your heart and set your affection on things above, not on things on the earth. He will keep your heart and mind stayed on Him.

The Joint-Heirs

The Millionaires and Joint Heirs
To The Kingdom Of God

Genesis 22:14; Exodus 17:15; Deuteronomy 32:30; Hebrews 11; Leviticus 26; 1 Peter 32; Habakkuk 3:3; Job 36; Hosea 11; Romans 8; Galatians 3; 1 John 3; Psalm 51; Deuteronomy 29; 1 King 3; 1 King 10; 2 Chronicles; Psalm 112; Psalm 132; 2 Corinthians 1; 2 Timothy; Revelations 12; 1 John 1; Hebrews 10:19; Revelations 1; Nehemiah 8; 1 Chronicles 29; Isaiah 60:19-20; Revelations 21:3; Proverbs 11; Philippians 4; Ephesians 1; Psalm 24; 1 Corinthians 10; 2 Samuel 22; Psalm 18; Psalm 143; Proverbs 8

The rich get richer and the poor folks are getting poorer desolated in spirit, decreasing in strength, and power. Sadly, we look at the revenues of others and wonder how they can have so much and God's children so little. You see, God's calculation in math will never be the same as humanity. Paper excites them, but their health, strength, and power continue to fade away. God's people are joint heirs to his Kingdom. Our acceptance into his family is predestinated to us into the adoption of children by Jesus Christ, according to the good pleasure of his will. God's people are the millionaires, and joint heirs to the Kingdom of God, the earth is the Lord's, and the fulness thereof; the world, and they that dwell therein. Even the world has not a portion in our inheritance.

Riches of His Glory

The depth of the riches are both wisdom and knowledge of God! All the riches which God has taken from the wicked that is ours, and our children's. Our King has enriched us with great riches, and we are His prince and princess. And if children, then heirs; heirs of God, and joint-heirs with Christ; if so be that we suffer with him, that we may also be glorified together. Adopted sons and daughters are royalty, more valuable than precious stones. The power of God keeps us through faith unto salvation. Our faith is tried refined by the fire-polished to perfection. For a season, were we in heaviness through manifold temptations where the trial of our faith, was much more precious than of gold? Though it was tried with fire, our praise and honor were to glory for the presence of Jesus Christ. His power is exemplified in the riches of his glory and the honour of his excellent majesty for eternity.

Riches and Honor

Both riches and honor come from our Father, the same Father of Abraham, Isaac, and Jacob. He reigns Supreme. There is no other God like him all over the world. In his hand is power and might, and if we are Christ's, then we are Abraham's seed, and heirs according to the promise. Jesus Christ reigns above all, and in his hand is power and might. His hand makes great and gives strength to all His people. Our richest cannot be told we are the millionaires and joint heirs to the Kingdom of God. We are adopted sons and daughters of the promise depending upon the King that is the King of all Kings. In his promises, your richness lies in his glory. No one can take it. No one can see it. You are rich in the power of God. You are rich in the blood of Jesus Christ. You are rich in the treasures of your heart, and you are rich in the word of God because you are the true millionaire, the joint heirs to the Kingdom of God.

Riches in Joy

Listen! When they look around and see God's people, they wonder why we have joy. They would never understand it. Then, they look at our life and ask—,

How do we live?
How do we make it?

No one would ever know because they cannot see the riches which God has given us.

No! They cannot understand the grace which saved us. Neither will they understand, how Jesus saved us; for these reasons, we serve Him. No! They cannot understand; why we are the true millionaires. No one would ever understand; we are joint heirs to the Kingdom of God. We have rendered joy, as we share our portions with them who have nothing. We do not want for anything; neither are we sorry because the joy of the LORD is our strength. With a perfect and generous heart, the Children of God rejoices as we give to the House of the LORD.

The world cannot understand the richness of his glory.
The world cannot understand the richness of his honor.
The world cannot understand the richness of his joy.
The world cannot understand He is God,
and besides Him, there is no other.
They cannot understand why Jesus Christ
will never fail or forsake his people.

Rich in Grace

Our riches are more than what they can see, the land in which we walk upon reaches far wide meeting at the four corners of the world. No one will understand how we own islands in continents and countries no man has traveled or the mountains no man has climbed. We are strangers dwelling in places none could bear. The world cannot understand the richness of liberty. We are justified by his grace; we are made joint-heirs according to the hope of eternal life, which is in Jesus Christ. So, we bear the pangs of sorrow and the afflictions from grief. We are rich with mercy and sufficient in grace.

Rich in Peace

Jehovah Shalom He is the God of our peace. We are not ignorant, or void of wisdom; but is despised and hated by man. The Holy Ghost granted us understanding; thus, we have learned to hold our peace. It is counted wise unto the Children of God. A closed mouth honors us with silence and increases our understanding. As the world rants and inflict their tyranny; we have the peace of God, which passes all understanding, and will keep our hearts and minds through Christ Jesus.

Rich in Provisions

When God provided Abraham a sacrifice for his son Isaac. Abraham called the place Jehovah Jireh. The world will never understand how God makes something out of nothing. When He hear the cry of his people. We are the Millionaire and joint heirs to the Kingdom of God. We return with much riches unto our tents, with much meat, silver, gold, brass, iron, and with raiment (clothing). Jehovah Jireh our God supplies our every need.

> The world cannot understand the richness of his grace.
> The world cannot understand the richness of his peace.
> The world cannot understand the richness of his provisions.
> The world cannot understand He is God,
> and besides Him, there is no other.
> They cannot understand why Jesus Christ
> will never fail or forsake his people.

Rich in The Presence of God

They look around at the victories won. They pounder in their thoughts, how can we afford such great armies. After defeating the Amalekites, Moses built an altar and called it Jehovah-Nissi, the lord of my banner. They wonder how we can afford such large armies when they do not understand the battles won. It is because Jesus promised to be our banner. How should one chase a thousand, and two put ten thousand to flight, except their Rock had sold them, and the Lord had shut them up? Neither can they understand the training we received. We only need five to chase a hundred, and an hundreds of us will put ten thousand to flight: and our enemies will fall before us because of the Word of God. It speaks volumes and uplifts His people and cuts off the enemy from beginning to end by the sword. We are the millionaires, the joint heirs to the Kingdom of God. We are trained to win and not fall.

By your standards, he becomes the banner as we express in words our interest in congregating to call him as a warning against the enemy. Our praises alert Him of lingering dangers as His presence remains as our defense mechanism. Equally important it is our duty to customize the faith and trust in his power. His glory covered the heavens, and the earth is full of his praise. Build an altar in your heart to honor the God of Salvation. An altar of sacrifice, for Jehovah-Nissi—The Lord is our banner. His power and presence make us triumphant against the enemy. They cannot understand why we are rich in His praises. It is because we exalt the name of Jesus Christ, for He delivered his flock from amongst the adversary. Therefore, put in practice the word and the promises of God so, he may shield us from diverse temptations.

The world cannot understand the richness in the presence of God.
The world cannot understand He is God
and besides Him there is no other.
They cannot understand why Jesus Christ
will never fail or forsake his people.

We are millionaires and joint-heirs To the Kingdom of God. Spiritually, adopted sons and daughters, a chosen generation, a royal priesthood, a holy nation, a peculiar people; that shows forth the praises to Jesus Christ. He has called us out of darkness into his marvellous light.

Riches in Testimony

We rejoice in the way of the testimonies, as much as in all richness. We talk about the miraculous works wrought amongst His people. The Holy Ghost taught the testimonies of old how he delivered many out of the hand of their enemies. His Word forever established in the hearts of them that trusted in His refuge. Many speak of the Laws of God receiving testimonies sealing that God is faithful and true. Our children are trained to keep His covenant and testimonies; to share with future generations forevermore. Today's moment of truth is for the rejoicing in all testimonies of our conscience. The heart reminds us that in simplicity and sincerity, we spiritually make known the wisdom and the grace of God. In our conversation to the world, we testify of Jesus Christ more abundantly. Never be ashamed of your testimony; regardless of its size, never be ashamed of the testimony of our Lord.

Richness in His Blood

They wonder why we turned away from a life of darkness. Trading partners for one who will walk with us in the light because we are no longer children of the dark. So we walk in the light, as our King is in the light, and we have fellowship one with another, and the blood of Jesus Christ cleanses us from all sin. The old life we knew was traded for one that is eternal, never fading away. Thus, we are overcome by the blood of the Lamb and by the word of our testimony. We tell the world, Jesus Christ has purged us with hyssop, and we are clean, washed, and made whiter than snow. So, we have the boldness to enter into the holiest by the blood of Jesus. We are given authority to seek after him at the Throne of Mercy, to call upon him, and relay our petitions and supplications. He has washed us from our sins in his blood,

The world cannot understand the richness of his testimonies.
The world cannot understand the richness in His Blood
The world cannot understand He is God and
besides Him, there is no other.
They cannot understand why Jesus Christ
will never fail or forsake his people

Rich in Salvation

We are rich in the salvation of Jesus Christ, heirs of Salvation, the righteousness of God. By acceptance of his resurrection, the bloodshed for washing away of all sins. The LORD has given us the shield of his salvation: and his kindness made us great. Against the world, he is our rock, fortress, deliver, our God, our strength, and in Him do we place all our trust. He is the buckler, the horn of our salvation, and high tower. In Him, the righteous can find a resting place. He is Jehovah Tsidkenu, the Lord our righteousness who restores all which we lost. Thus, we offer the sacrifices of righteousness, and to do according to the commandments. We put our trust in the LORD. He makes our ways straight and the Holy Ghost quickens our spirit. As we hearken to his voice, The Lord brings our soul out of trouble and leads us in righteousness. All riches and honor belong to the LORD, the God of our salvation. In him, we have durable riches and righteousness.

Rich in Vision

Jehovah Shamma, the LORD, is there ready to quench the violence of fire, blocking fiery darts of the enemy, and making the weak strong, they grew into brave fighters that put to flight the armies of the enemy. Our vision is the richness of the Holy Ghost, who led us from the cords of affliction. With bands of love, he removes the yoke of oppression. The world looks around and wonders about these things, for they have underestimated the strength of God's people.

Riches in Wisdom

Jesus Christ has given us wisdom and knowledge. Because we inquire at his hand, he also has given us riches, wealth, and honour. We believe and trust in the Laws of God, as we distinctively read, receiving the sense to understand the precepts written. The richness that man has cannot save or buy them peace of mind. For the powers of God, conquers the mire destinies established by small armies. Continuously, they confuse themselves in the heart and mind. The riches are in the divine name of Jesus Christ. His life, no man can own neither control.

The world cannot understand the richness of salvation.
The world cannot understand the richness in Vision.
The world cannot understand the richness in wisdom.
The world cannot understand He is God,
and besides Him, there is no other.
They cannot understand why Jesus Christ
will never fail or forsake his people

The world can never understand the faith the reigns in the heart of God's people. But we will not be stingy. Instead, we invite them to share our wealth. For the LORD has says to split the wealth of enemy amongst the brethren. Our inheritance is incorruptible and cannot be stolen by greed and corruption. The world cannot take away our millions; it is reserved in a place called heaven.

The world cannot understand the richness of his glory.
The world cannot understand the richness of his honor.
The world cannot understand the richness of his joy.
The world cannot understand the richness of his grace.
The world cannot understand the richness of his peace.
The world cannot understand the richness of his provisions
The world cannot understand the richness in the presence of God.
The world cannot understand the richness of his testimonies.
The world cannot understand the richness in His Blood
The world cannot understand the richness of salvation.
The world cannot understand the richness in Vision.
The world cannot understand the richness in wisdom.
The world cannot understand He is God,
and besides Him, there is no other.
They cannot understand why Jesus Christ
will never fail or forsake his people

We are millionaires and joint heirs to the Kingdom of God. Spiritually, adopted sons and daughters, a chosen generation, a royal priesthood, a holy nation, a peculiar people; that shows forth the praises to Jesus Christ. He has called us out of darkness into his marvellous light.

As we keep His commandments and do them, we will prosper in all that we do. The wealth and riches remain in our house because his righteousness endures forever.

Keep Moving Forward
in Boldness

Children of God
Hebrews 10; Psalm 46; 1 John 3

God's love honors the believers because the unbeliever knows him not. The world cannot perceive the love of God; they are polluted by common calamities. The manner of love bestowed upon the children of God knows they are entitled to the blessings of God. The world cannot accept the greatness of Jesus Christ because they lack knowledge of knowing him.

We are the sons of God; we are privileged to be called a Child of God and we have his Spirit in us. As joint-heirs to His Kingdom, it is our duty to walk by faith, live by hope, and trust in him. As chosen vessels carrying the Word of God, it is of great importance to resemble him in All Likeness (Mentally and Spiritually). The word says, it does not yet appear what we should be: but we know that when he appears, we should be like him.

To begin the manifestation, we must be purified and washed through the Gospel of Truth. It will purify, free the inward man from anything that debases, pollutes, adulterates, or contaminates. Simply, choose to separate yourself and cling to righteousness. Strive for perfection – remain free from guilt and sin. The unfaithful turns from serving the LORD. They have chosen to entangle themselves with lustful addictions. Others have this hope; that by the sanctification of our faith and salvation; we are called Children of God. We know the LORD is pure and holy. As such, we must present ourselves as holy and acceptable. Letting the words of our mouth, and the meditation of our heart, be acceptable in the sight, O Lord, our strength, and our redeemer.

As you spiritually mature, express love and shun envy. Let us not murder the character of others struggling to keep the faith. Neither their personality nor defiles one another image. From the beginning, we were taught to love, show mercy, and obey the commandments. Hatred knows not mercy and lacks compassion for any. When you aim to destroy a persons' life; you have chosen to slay their image. Assassinating everything, they worked hard to build and ruining relationships. Some folks cannot accept rejection and find ways to retaliate or go into hiding.

Children of God should not do this to one another and should try to understand the emotions of others.

Doing so means understanding the love of God, and why he would give his life for us. He did not think twice. Instead, he said, Sacrifice and offering was no longer accepted by him and could never make us perfect. Hence, a body the Father prepared for His Son Jesus Christ, who became the perfect sacrifice to redeem and set free. In our ministry, we ought to lay down our lives for the others by neglecting your life to perform or provide services for others. Whoso has the world's good (having worldly possessions such as food, clothing, shoes, and etcetera's); and see your brother (body of Christ and natural family members) have need and you do not share or have compassion for them, how does the love of God dwell in you?

Try to obey the commandments written and apply the doctrine of Jesus Christ to your life. Practice setting good Christian standards, which would draw others near to God. The unsaved is always looking at the lifestyle of the Children of God. So, try hard to seek after holiness, and when you find yourself falling; ask for help because God is our refuge and strength, a very present help in trouble. What manner of love the Father has given us that we should be called sons of God (Children of God). The world does not know us because we are no longer partakers of darkness. They knew not Jesus Christ in the pardon of their sins. Observe to do all the things of the laws of righteousness because we are Children of the most High God.

The River of living waters
Ezekiel 47; Jeremiah 17; John 7; Psalm 104

The holy waters flows from the heart it flows signifying the law and the word of God as we stand firmly upon the foundation Up its surface life desires the mind of its creator woolly pouring out in spiritual sacrifices of prayers and praise what is there to offer to a living God an empty vessel desperately in need a reformation.

We falter when deciding to go in the opposite direction. Instead of promoting the service of God witnessing, or sharing the gospel with others, we choose to do the opposite. Without reasoning many find it hard to move forward. It should instead seem second nature for those that have walked the faith for so long. Everyone must show themselves to be of the same in Jesus Christ. Many are willing to serve, But without the pains and sufferings. We find it most difficult to enter into giving a praise. When so much time is wasted and taking and selfish acts of disobedience. There is a great injustice for us to enter into his presence as filthy rags.

The Lord would not have his people ridiculed with such confusion. He grants us the opportunity to meditate, attain his word, repent, and not to go back to our old lifestyles. To sustain, we are commanded to encourage the feeble to stand. Saints of God are to stand tall as trees bearing righteous fruit which is produced from the seed (Word); planted in the heart. A assembly, drawing from the well of living waters, and streams from Lebanon. Spiritual wealth and beauty; trees of the LORD set in place to help others build stronger foundations. By virtue and maturity in Jesus Christ, we have diversity of gifts which are for the edification of the Church. So, we draw our strength and nutrients from the Holy Ghost who is given to honor the LORD our God.

On either side of ministry in or outside the Church walls, should grow all types of trees because of the abiding in Jesus Christ. In him, our leaves will never fade, and the souls brought to the House of God will not be consumed. They have learned to draw courage, build hope, faith, and trust in the Creature of all things. Faith increases, by hearing and hearing the Word of God. Streams of waters flow from the sanctuary because many thirst for the holiness and sanctification. There is a hunger to experience a touch of God, whether through prayer, praise, worship, or the Gospel of Jesus Christ. His Word is the leaf of medicine to ease pain and soothe afflictions.

The rivers of living water flows from deep within the soul. At the river, your life must be grounded and yielding (bringing forth) good fruit. Therefore, the Saints of God can find hope in the LORD, the fountain of living waters. As the scripture is written to believe on the Lord and out of the belly will flow rivers of living water. Allow the Word of God, to pour out in the presence of God and your ministry to spread forth. Align lifestyle to mirror Holiness, planted by the LORD to stand strong and unwavering like as the cedar trees of Lebanon. Those belonging to Jesus Christ are full of the sap of (His Word); grounded and planted by his hand to mature and follow after what is good and acceptable. Strive to become as a tree planted by the waters, grounded in the perfection of righteousness, spreading the Gospel of Truth.

Reaching Out For Acceptance By Men
Galatians 1, Galatians 2

Rather saved or unsaved many set their endeavors to become accepted by others. A world filled with the outcast of those that prey on the confused and less fortunate. To overturn their foundation. They persuade the weak to desert the true gospel drawing them away until realization sets in and the bar is too high to reach.

Be comfortable with whom you are in the body of Christ. Your fingerprint is a unique identity and symbolizes there is only one you. Set your afflictions on pleasing God. For it is from your mother's womb that he ordained and chose you to do good works that are designed for your accomplishments.

Why look for approval from others? Will it merit you as righteous? If Jesus has called you, than he has ordained and crafted you to perform your duties. Wait for the Lord to equip and promote you to the place of acceptance. The Lord must perform the transformation of character and give you an unction from the Holy Spirit. Do not allow corrupt thoughts to discourage your Salvation. It is the Lord that qualifies and imparts extraordinary gifts in the heart to help as a way of providing divine instructions to the one that is commissioned.

Do not be removed or forfeit your belief for those who perverts the gospel of Jesus Christ. Continue to publish and profess your position and dependence upon Him. Some of us are deeply affected by how others may perceive our character. Physically, we grow and become concerned with the thoughts of others than with the matters of our Faith. Naturally enslaved to the perceptions other. Exposing ourselves to their vicious attacks and shallow minds.

Stop reaching out for acceptance by man. Do not forfeit your Salvation or trade it for unwise counsel. Recover your identity in the Lord and allow the inward comfort of your heart to freely submit to the oracles of God. True believers depend upon the efficacy and acceptance of Jesus Christ. The world is addicted to sin. As a result, do not reach out for their acceptance when it deals with your Salvation. Receive your teachings and instructions from the Holy Ghost which will bring to remembrance all things that you have studied and learned. Believe in the infinite excellence of the God that you serve. Only he can validate your purpose. You are a vessel, an instrument separated for use (not of men, neither by man, but the Father, Son, and Holy Ghost.

This present evil world is addicted to sin. It cannot accept who you are in the body of Christ . In what manner could a man profit from perverting the gospel to lead those who are feeble and desolate. It takes the Lord to transform the heart and imagination of all. Ignore the opinions and attitudes of other. Your duty is not to please man but to persuade them.

God has already chosen and given you revelation and knowledge why seek the approval of another? They cannot transform your life or purpose. There are some who would try hard to alter the plans given to you. Salvation is a special adaptation towards righteousness. Obey the instruction from the Holy Ghost and excel in your SALVATION. Man cannot validate, "who you are, neither your purpose." Look to Jesus Christ the Author and Finisher of your FAITH.

Do Not Waver in Your Thoughts
2 Thessalonians 2; Hebrews 10; James 1; James 4; Mark 9

Be not shaken in your mind. Do not ponder in your thoughts for those who are weak, in their faith, will fall victim to deception. In high honors and regards to holiness, we must esteem and encourage one another to remain steadfast in our faith with much prayer and fasting. Pretenders have a zeal for God and his glory but have defiantly established a platform for themselves. They sit back, waiting for an opportunity to act mischievous or cause another to err. The doctrine of Jesus Christ is the only true gospel. Studying prepares us to acknowledge what is right and aligns with the Word of God. Thus, we ought not to be deceived, confused about our duties, devotion to Jesus Christ or the miraculous works performed. Also, studying enlightens our understanding and guards against false doctrines and corrupt teachings. These are tactics used to victimize the Body of Christ.

From one Sunday to another, many Saints do not pick up the bible to read it. During Sunday morning worship and praise, they perform their praise break. Afterward, many are too tired to even turn to the scripture readings, nor do they take notes. Instead of trusting God, many trust the spoken words of the speaker. As a result, many falter at the promises of God and can barely make it through the week.

There is so much to read and meditate in the Bible. The LORD is always speaking from scripture to scripture. We lose the power of the anointing by constantly diminishing the light present within our bodies. The Holy Ghost is willing to give us every tool to defeat the enemy. However, some refuse to put in the work and simply settle for the residue left behind by the Holy Ghost. I desire the full strength and not the water down version of the Gospel of Truth. It is good to hear the truth about your commitment to the Gospel and receive correction now. Every Saint knows Jesus Christ is the "real deal." Yet, we pretend to don't know anything because it is easier to forget than to remember.

On the other hand, there are the "faithful few," who will trust Jesus Christ against the odds, never wavering in their faith. If God said it, that settles it, and all is well with their soul. Those are the people to include within your inner circle. Surround yourself with a seasoned Saint that has a real relationship with the LORD and speaks the truth even when it hurts. The title says, "Do not waver in your thoughts." To survive spiritually, you cannot align yourself with Saints that are still drinking milk. Instead, connect with a Saint that is feasting on meat because they will best understand your position and struggles.

Salvation is not easy, and it requires obedience and sacrifices. What are you sacrificing? Well, it entails trading in your secular values for holiness and sanctification. You are giving up a lifestyle of sin to walk upright before the Lord. Listen, Friend, you will fall many times, but always get back up, repent, and keep moving. Jesus Christ has given us the Holy Ghost, which teaches us everything according to the Gospel of Truth. However, you must be ready and willing to receive all that it has to offer. Be attentive to the teachings of God's Word and make an effort to obey the commandments. A seasoned Christian is firmly grounded in the Word of God. Thus, they try to hold fast to their profession and faith without wavering. They understand the faithfulness and promises of God.

There are deformities in many Christian churches, and Saints of God do stumble in their walk. Instead of holding on, they let go and blame the LORD for their failures. I tell you the truth, if and when you fall, please, get up, dust yourself off, and keep going. Keep the faith and trust that Jesus Christ can and will help you prevail against the enemy. Life is not fair, and it gives a variety of blows to cripple the Children of God. Do not give up, and do not waver in your thoughts. Those who give up and turn from serving Jesus Christ should blame themselves for letting go. They become angry with the Lord, shut themselves off from other Saints, and grow defiant towards the Word of God.

If you find yourself with your back up against the wall, come out the corner praising and exalting the Name of Jesus Christ. It is okay to cry your way through the trial. Trust me—it is okay, and if someone tells you differently, then they are not a good friend. Do not let your fleshly desires get the best of you. Doing so could jeopardize you missing out on the blessings of the Lord. Touch your mind, and say, "Let this mind be in me, which is also in Christ Jesus." Stand strong and worship the Mighty God.

Friend, worry about who you are and where you are going in the Lord. The world takes care of its own, they are all pretenders, unrealistic, and there is no ground for security, only unforeseen wars. Cling not to the coat tale of desperation where there is no peace. For it is engaging in the act of war designed to trip and plan downfalls. There are always wolves, waiting to seduce the weak without knowledge or power. Wolves feed on the uncontrollable desires of vulnerable Saints. These are reasons to pair yourself with stronger Saints and spend less time with unsaved friends. You do not have to cut them off. Simply let them know you have a new partner, and his name is Jesus Christ.

When your friend laughs, it is okay—let them. You see, this is where new "Saint's of God," or "Babes in Christ," err. Do not move back into the grips of sin. Mistakenly, they believe the world can change them; but at what cost. By fault, they get caught up in the web of deceit, which is an unwise pursuit of happiness and will quickly fade.

Waver not in your thoughts but focus more on what is from and of God. Do not waver in your thoughts. Instead, use your faith to ask what you desire from the LORD and believe you will receive. Wavering symbolizes an unstable mind driven with the wind and tossed back and forth because it is confused and without instructions.

Build your mind upon the elements using prayer, fasting, and worshipping. Find scriptures to meditate on daily. A wavering mind is a double-minded person, unstable in all their ways. It is unpleasing to the Lord. The word of God warrants peace, but his people need to desire peace. Do not allow your faith to vanish because it lacks the knowledge of God. Allow the Holy Ghost to take charge, and it will train your thoughts to think about the value of your salvation. Continue to draw closer to Jesus, and he will draw closer to you. Profess unto the LORD, that he may cleanse your hands and purify your heart.

The Lord does things according to his will. He is exalted and magnified above all things. Like a whirlwind, he destroys and has overthrown the wicked, and they cannot escape His judgment. The wind has bound them up in her wings; thus, they are all ashamed. Their thoughts have troubled their souls, and peace is destroyed.

In contrast, the wise will shine as the brightness of the firmament. For their knowledge has increased. There is a select few who are purified, made white, and tried through the fire. Hear the word of the Lord? The Lord has a controversy against his people, and they are lying in spiritual poverty. There is no truth, mercy, or knowledge of God. Without fear, they strive with the Gospel of Truth, and slowly perish and are destroyed. Many despise righteousness and have rejected the laws of God. Jesus Christ is your Redeemer, and all that we endure should not separate us from the love of God. Hold on to His love and kindness. Learn to worship him for His Excellency. Continue your relationship with him and have confidence that he would deliver by his power and precious blood. Never waver in your faith. If you find yourself in disbelief, say, "Lord, I believe; help thou mine unbelief."

That Is What I Do

Deuteronomy 10:12; Deuteronomy 13:4; Colossians 2:6;
Proverbs 3: 5-7; Micah 6:8; Zechariah 7:9; Deuteronomy 4:39;
Ecclesiastes 12:13; 1 Corinthians 15; 1 King 2; 1 Samuel 25;
Philippians 4:7; Hebrews 13; Malachi 3; John 4; John 16

When we converse with others, everyone wants to exchange dialogue and keep the lines of communication going. During the conversation, we find ourselves bragging about family, friends, and life's experiences. On occasions, we may bump into an old friend and reminisce on old memories, have a few laughs, share life-changing events, skills, talents, and expertise.

Now, consider the end of the conversations? Did everyone walk away with a smile or a frown? Or, maybe, there were awkward moments or feelings; knowing the person was untruthful. In a short period, life résumés are disclosed and very descriptive. What could you have possibly said to deflate their ego? Maybe, present your résumé of diverse accomplishments? How could you share your success in Jesus Christ without boasting? Or, share the essential benefits and high statue of a Saint of God? After all, only Jesus Christ knows the Truth. His truth changes not; he is the same God of Abraham, Isaac, and Jacob. Jesus Christ is the same yesterday, and today, and forever. He is the Lord, who changes not.

When you are alone, you sit and think about life accomplishments. Wondering what have you accomplished? So, you ask, "Lord, what is my role? Or, what have I accomplished in you?" Spiritually, you hear a small voice, whisper in your ear, "What does the LORD require of you?" The Holy Ghost reminds you of your position in Jesus Christ. With an astonished face, you say, "That Is What I Do!"

This Is What I do! I strive towards becoming a master builder and laying a foundation upon the Rock of Salvation. By His grace, I am what I am; for day and night, do I labor in the abundance of his love. My soul inquiries to know the good and gain what is profitable—obeying the oracles as spoken by His chosen vessels. All are commissioned to keep the charge of the Lord, walking in relationship with the Holy Ghost, observing his statutes, commandments, judgments, and testimonies. I fear The LORD, respecting him in total submission, and giving reverence for his Omnipotence because authority and power reign with the presence of His Glory and is infinite. In such great love, we yearn to build a relationship with all our heart, soul, and mind. There is nothing created or completed without him. Hence, we surrender in total dependence while patiently waiting for His Majesty because He is God alone.

He gives prosperity to all who do whatsoever he commands. Jesus sent Peace to encamp like an invisible soundproof bubble. She does not hear when the disturbance is knocking. Because she is there defending her sense of harmony and "Peace," is triumphing in war. She is counted as wise to those who speak not; thus, "Peace" passes all understanding, keeping hearts and minds through Christ Jesus.

This Is What I Do! After receiving Christ Jesus, the LORD, I walk in upright in His presence day and night, worshipping him in spirit and truth. The Spirit of Truth guides me into all truth, never speaking of himself. Instead, he says whatsoever, he hears from the Master and shows me the more excellent things to come.

This Is What I Do! I execute truth and fairness when judging others. Showing concern for their needs and showing compassion to others suffering in distress. The calamities appear more than what they can bear. So, this is what I do, judging them not while soothing the pain with encouraging words of wisdom. It is good to do right by others and embrace compassion and walking humbly before the Lord Our God.

This is what I do, trust in the LORD with all my heart and lean not into my understanding. Secular wisdom is limited, for it never acknowledges the ways of righteousness. So, I choose to follow the path directed by the Holy Ghost; it teaches how not to be wise in your own eyes. Instead, fear the LORD, and turn from sin. You are royalty, and wicked men will not understand your behavior and speech. Their speech deceives the hearts of the simple. So, "This Is What I Do!" I came not with excellency of speech or of wisdom, declaring to you the testimony of God.

Consider what is in your heart and shout to the world, the LORD he is God in heaven above, and there is none to compare. "This Is What I Do!" I serve Jesus Christ. Hear the conclusion of the whole matter. Let all fear God, keep his commandments; this is our duty.

Backed up Against the Wall, Troubled on Both Sides

Exodus 13:3, 8, 14,17, 19, 21-22; Exodus 14:10, 13-15

Remember the day in which you were delivered? You told everyone how you made it through the storms and rain. You probably exaggerated a little to spruce up the story. How the wind blew your umbrella upward, and strong winds almost pulled you from under your covering. Maybe, you were in a ditch so deep, you felt as if there was no way out and wanted to give up. Or maybe the floods were so high that you almost drowned in your tears. Backed up against the wall, seeing trouble on both sides, you looked up, and there was God.

Living in the City of Egypt, your soul wandered in the plains of wilderness. There, you lay in the House of Bondage, confused and desolate. Your offering is the sounds of moaning, yearning for a way of escape. If there is a little room, possibly you could wiggle your way through the cracks and crevasses. But, shame and embarrassment block the light, so you cannot see your way around the wall.

Jesus looked upon the countenance of your heart and saw the wholeness thereof, reached down, and pulled you from the grips of despair. He instructed you to tell others why you chose to serve Him. Tell the testimonies to them that will hear of His Glory.

So, you begin to tell the story on "how you were "Backed up Against the Wall, Troubled on Both Sides," and Jesus Christ; saved you. The armor of God was removed, and you let your guard down for a minute or two. As a result, you were not fit for war or the battles that rose against you.

The LORD God gave deliverance from bondage. Since you failed to obey the commandments and would not turn from temptation, he allowed you to fall into captivity. Disobedience made you vulnerable and prey to the enemy because you did not learn how to fight against temptation. Amid the tribulations, the Holy Ghost promised; God will not lead you in the same direction or cause you to falter in your faith.

Because He knows our strengths and weaknesses. God's Word Will Come to Pass. So, take the time to Acknowledge the act of God's promise that he would visit and bring you out. It is an encouragement to your faith. Stand up, hold on, and do not give up on Hope in the Glory of The Almighty. The Presence of God will continuously go before us day or night to give us security and peace. Even when you are backed up against the wall, troubled on both sides, come out with your hands lifted up and your mouth filled with praises. The Lord will hear you and hide you in his pavilion.

We Are Winners
and Never Losers

Never Mind the Scars, Touch the Heart
John 1

A wounded soul is like trying to find a lost needle in a haystack. Life's afflictions forced them to camouflage their scars. You are highly favored and endowed with the strength and the outpouring of his anointing, which ignites our spirit. Because of this, we are alive and secluded in his presence. Uniquely, the transformation produces a glorious light that will shine during this imprudent generation. Albeit, they will never know why it exists. When chosen, Jesus Christ gave us instruction to teach the gospel to a dying Nation. There is a famine in the land, and the lost are starving for love, mercy, and grace. Often, they are overlooked while their hearts ache for someone to hug and care for them. We cannot save everybody or anybody. However, we are equipped to introduce them to Jesus Christ.

Their hurts are an illustration of the wounds. Wounds that never seem to heal. So, they mirror the visible scars. A weary soul only knows what it is accustomed to seeing and hearing. If their environment or surroundings never changes, all will remain captivated by the same things that are visualized every day. Agreeable, the world has a mixture of actors, actresses, con artists, beggars, and fakers. Never mind the scars, touch their hearts, share with them the good news of Jesus Christ. If you stare at the scars to long, the wounded will not accept the Word of God. In comparison to others, in their hearts, they may believe you are judging them on what you see.

Sadly, because of their appearance, many Christians will not bother sharing a conversation with them. "Hello, and a Smile" is free. Scars do not always have to be about their flaws or mistakes. There are a host of reasons, and only God knows. Our role is to get them to believe that Christ is real and to encourage them to come and visit. I was glad when they said to me; let us go into the house of the LORD. So, never mind the scars, touch the heart to come and sit in the presence of God, even if it is for a second or two.

Scars

When you attended the first day of school, preferably middle or high school. It was not easy to meet and make new friends. However, you were approached, the introduction were given, and today, you have a new friend. What if you were attending a new school and desperately needed directions to your class, and no one helps? How would you feel?

Such a moment would remain with you for a lifetime. In Similarity, this is probably how those in the world might feel. It takes strong Christians to interact with the community. Take this same demonstration and substitute the person for a lost soul that you feel is not approachable. Regardless of who they are or the lifestyle, possibly the scars are badges of honor. For this cause, we have to be strong and sure that Christ has called us to minister to such souls.

Remember, some scars are surgically removed, and others are deeply branded in the heart. But, the LORD God always places someone in your life to help you through the storms. They become audio diaries that listen, and hopefully, they will maintain your secrets.

Sometimes, it takes others to let us know what our self-worth is. Cloudy circumstances and penetrating hurts clog our ears and stains our hearts. We cannot hear the comforting words spoken by the mouth of God; neither can we receive the healing powers of love. Desperately, the soul reaches out as it slowly sinks deeply into a dark hole. Mental scars are harder to erase, and it seems impossible to forgive. Many Christians are wounded individuals tattooed with invisible scars that are naked to the eyes. The more they continue to push forward, beyond the infirmities, God strengthens their stance. First, understand life battles should never define your character or how you feel about the Lord, Jesus Christ. He is faithful to His Word and will never forsake or leave you naked. The love of Jesus Christ covers and takes away life's reproach. So, lookup, keep walking in Him, press towards the victory flag and praise God each step of the way.

Exquisitely You

Hey, wake up!

Downtrodden, stuck in the gutter, why are you so fluttered

Laughter, laughter, laughter it slaughters the wickedness that tries to still your joy

I don't know about you and them.

But, I do know that I cannot swim in the pool of disdain things that seem insane.

What is wrong with all these people?

Have they not, do they not, must they not, understand the realistic powers of God's mighty hand.

Put my head down, lift my head, walk around town, dance up and down.

What shall I do, or what shall I say?

They have me here, so, where should I stay.

Stay with Jesus Christ!

Never let go regardless – "Oh, No!"

What was I told?

Jesus hid me deep in the fold.

He hid me in the fold of his pocket, in the fold of his hand, under his wings, and snuggly tucked away from those evil things again.

Shadows are dark, and pains are hard, but never will I let down my guard.

I turned around just for a moment, and then I turned the other way just for a moment

All the turning and turning churned my thoughts, and now I think I am a little lost.

Lost for words, wishing I could fly away like a bird.

Fly, high in the sky, into the realms of holiness.

Yep, they want to be me; they wish they were me, but no one can be me because only I can be me.

Empty pockets, Jesus Christ, will clock it, and no one can block it.

My thoughts are sometimes pure and occasionally; impure.

Yet, I struggle with life's intuition and strive to perfect my weaker conditions.

Well, chill, heal, fill, and deal with your insecurities and identities.

You know who you are, you know what you need, and do you care about your place in space.

Fill your heart with things that are certain and move a little to the right and pull on heaven's curtain.

Pull hard until it opens, stand still, and watch Jesus send down tokens.

Tokens of love

Tokens of happiness

Tokens of wisdom

Tokens of understanding

Tokens of Him

Tokens of well just about every heavenly treasure.

Look up high into the sky, squinch your eyes a little and just fly.

Don't think about your inabilities or vulnerabilities

Run like a jaguar and run like a cheetah,

Run as fast as you can even if it feels like you're, running in slow motion.

As time passes, you will see the extra miles trained, and the strength and power gained.

You are perfect just the way you are.

Look in the mirror and turn around, tweak your inner soul to resemble the scriptures of old.

You are exquisite and of glorious perfection.

Indeed, continue to trust Jesus Christ!

Just watch and see.

I Wanna Be More Like JESUS

Keeping It Simple

Hebrew 12:14; St. John 3:3; Romans 10:9; Luke 15:7-10; Romans 10:9; Matthew 3:13-17; Galatians 3:27; 1 Corinthians 12:13; 1 John 2:6; Philippians 2:2

As Children of God, it is our duty to "Emulate" Jesus and strive to be more like him in every aspect of our life. To Be More Like Jesus; is deemed as to without spot or wrinkle. When we were younger, it did not take much to mimic the behavior of our parents or favorite family member. We studied them and knew what they would do or not do. So, we found the simplest thing in them to imitate, and it wasn't hard to do. Now, as Children of God, we are striving every day for perfection. We are trying so hard that we forget about the simple steps to take to increase our levels of spiritual maturity towards holiness.

Born Again

Born in the flesh is a "physical birth," and converted in the Spirit is a "spiritual birth." When God created us, he created humanity to resemble holiness. Born again means to repent and accept Jesus Christ as your Lord and Savior. Repentance opened the door for transformation. The Blood of Jesus cleanses and beautifies us, removing all filthiness and implementing the richness of mercy and grace. So many times, we look at ourselves and see that we are far from perfection. Yet, we have come so far in holiness and receiving full acceptance into God's family. Except a man be born again, he cannot see the kingdom of God.

Confessing unto Salvation

Speak up and speak loud, confess your faults before all, by allowing your soul to be the witness to your speech. Lift your voice, confess with your mouth, the Lord Jesus. You have shaken heaven because, for a second, may two, the Gospel of Truth has prevailed against disbelief. Now, the time has come for; as your heart receives the truth that God raised the Lord Jesus from the dead, and you are now SAVED. Let the heavens be glad, for joy is in heaven over one sinner that repented and received Jesus Christ: the GREAT GIFT OF SALVATION.

You are destined for greatness because you are on the LORD's side. The time has come to walk closely with the Holy Ghost; for he is given as a Comforter. Daily, he will teach you and bring all things to remembrance; whatsoever Jesus Christ has said to you. There is no room for doubt; neither do you have to think about what the scripture says. Pull up a chair, a small table, and a quiet little spot. Take the time to read, search the scriptures to know what the LORD is saying. Feed the mind, heart, and soul with the manna from On High. Let it take root and manifest in your life—a good work has begun in you, and the LORD is more than ready to smooth and fill all the broken crevasses. Heaven is rejoicing over you, a new addition to the family. You are on your way to becoming more like Jesus.

Baptized By Water (To Fulfill Righteousness)

Jesus came to John to be baptized to fulfill all righteousness, and when he came up from out of the water, the heavens were opened to him. The Spirit of God, which is the Holy Ghost, descended like a dove and lighting to him. The Lord Jesus went down to be washed with water, glory, and joy adorned him because his Father was well pleased with His Son. When you receive the baptism by water, the Father and Son give heavenly gifts to sustain your growth as you move forward with your salvation. The Holy Ghost descends, resting in your heart as the heavens open up; giving you boldness to enter into the holies of holies. Power and authority are granted unto those who receive and walk uprightly before the Lord Jesus Christ. The only God that reigns Supreme. Wake up to receive the gift of the Holy Ghost and fulfill righteousness. You are now a peculiar sheep, shaped for the Kingdom of God. Seek that which is good and walk obedient to the ordinances of Jesus Christ. Work hard, and form a life to be more like Jesus, one day at a time, not speedily or drastically. Simply take your time to commune and communicate with the God of Abraham, Isaac, and Jacob.

Redeemed By The Blood

The confession of sin and acceptance of Jesus Christ baptized you into Christ, and now you have put on Christ, immediately redeemed as both a servant and disciple in the body of Christ. As Children of God, we walk in newness of life with circumcised hearts. Your baptism brought you closer to becoming more like Jesus through faith in Christ because you were redeemed by The Blood.

By The Holy Ghost

Regardless of who you are, never mind the ethnicity, age, or SIN; Jesus Christ is ready to hear the most sincere prayer you have ready to give to Him. No one has the power to judge any for their past transgressions or iniquities. The LORD does not have respect of persons. By one Spirit, we are all baptized into one body, and all are made to drink into one Spirit. There is unity in Jesus Christ. How can two walks together unless they agree. If we walk together, all will understand their position and role in the Body of Christ. Abide and walk in obedience mimicking the path laid by Jesus. Train your mind to be in Christ Jesus—forever searching for strength, wisdom, and knowledge in the Power of His Might and in the beauty of his holiness. So, train your mind to think like Jesus Christ by reading and meditating on His. Grab a note pad, your best writing pen, and jot down your thoughts as you feast on the biblical pages of pureness. Let not your heart be troubled, neither be afraid to seek the wonderful treasures of God. He will fill your mind with much wisdom; simply trust and believe He can and he will.

Moreover, if you want to be more like Jesus, it is written, Be ye holy; for I am holy. You must be holy unto Jesus Christ, the Savior of your soul. Follow peace with all men. Without holiness, you cannot see the Lord. Strive to be Holy, because your holiness defines your position with God.

Every day, desire to Be More Like Him

Lord Renew My Mind In You

Recuperating

**Psalm 51:10; Isaiah 40:31; John 17:17 Isaiah 40:31;
Isaiah 33:2; Isaiah 41:1; Psalm 46:10; Romans 12:2;
2 Corinthians 4:16; Colossians 3:10; Titus 3:5**

When we have completed an exhausting task, we find ourselves quietly sitting down and dozing off to the quietness that sits still within our environment.

After returning home from an exasperating drive that seemed hours long, we find ourselves quietly sitting in the car. For a moment, we sit still resting our thoughts on the many miles that were traveled and how The LORD has kept us safe.

When we have lost our place, daydreaming, and wondering off in time, God resets our thinking and shakes us back into reality.

We find ourselves quietly sitting, wondering how to get back to the place of performing spiritual things. Those things that were appeasing to our LORD and Savior; that made Him smile upon us. How can we recoup (regain or recover) what we have lost? Many of us have lost the zeal or passion for Jesus Christ. Yes, we quickly make it known that He is our Master; but, we are slacking in our duties. Prayer has become minimized, love remains in abundance, sacrifices have minimized, exaltation has minimized, and Our communing with Jesus Christ is minimized.

Wait for the LORD

Those who fail to wait upon the LORD assumes that they have the power and ability to ascend far beyond their problems. They tend to think themselves are stronger than they are. So, they falter, faint, and utterly fall in their human-nature. "BY FAITH," we are to wait upon the LORD. The consciousness of the mind; makes us aware of our weaknesses. The Consciousness of the Mind being that of the HOLY GHOST, let us know: Jesus Christ will not fail, and His GRACE is sufficient. When you renew this mind – Strength is renewed, Anointing is renewed, Relationship is renewed, and My works in you are renewed. Because your body is the lamp which is supplied with fresh oil, so, allow the Holy Ghost to burn like fire in your Soul.

Clean Heart

Like King David, we sadly lament this unto Jesus Christ. We have the power to offer insincerity, "a cry for restoration." Your prayers acknowledge total dependency upon Him. There is Nothing to impossible for Jesus Christ. He Can if he desires to " Create in us a clean heart." Jesus Christ is full of "GRACE," and we are cleansed through the word. Therefore, allow the Word to sanctify you through the truth because His is truth and will never fail. Put away all things which so easily besets you and the disorder of our responsibilities that affects our spiritual life in Jesus Christ. We are not giving Him all that is within Our hearts, which should equate to one hundred percent. Allow the Lord to create in you a clean heart and renew a right spirit within. He can Repair what is broken on the inside. Whatever has caused a "Set-back," in your WALK with Him. Also, He can repair your inconsistencies linked to Conflicts, Discrepancies, and Contradictions. Slowly, yield to the power of the Holy Ghost and cry out to the LORD, *"Fix me and help me not to depart from you again."*

The LORD Is My Strength Every Morning

He is gracious to you; as you wait for him, in the mornings, the days of happiness, Jesus Christ remains as your strength and grace in times of trouble. Know then, His grace is sufficient, and He will never leave you without a shield of protection against the adverse elements of defeat. Joy comes in the morning, the Holy Ghost has opened your vision to see what has taken place and how the LORD has gained the victory. Never stop trusting in the strength of Jesus Christ; he can save you from the perils of life. Every morning, He gives you the strength to build and create testimonies for you to share His goodness and mercy for everlasting praise, glory, and honor.

Let the Holy Ghost renew your mind in Christ Jesus. A renewed mind – Gives Strength to soar upward and not downward. God's people do not have to keep "Crashing To The Ground." Instead, learn how to fly high above calamities. Press on and Press Through Adversities by increasing in perseverance and continually wait upon the LORD. In due season you will reap a great harvest of souls for the kingdom of God. Your testimonies will tell the stories of "how you made it over and through," it will encourage others to serve Jesus Christ.

Keep Silent

Keep silent before the LORD, sit still, and renew your strength by drawing near, communicating in righteousness. Present your problems for The Lord summons all to present their problems. No problem is out of his rule because He is Creator of Heaven and Earth. So, sit still and Keep Silent in the presence of God, and remain confident. The Unsaved will try hard to defend their opinions concerning your troubles. They will always have an answer for your problem and utterly FALTER in their words. When you do not understand, simply stand still and Keep Silent before the Lord Jesus. Be still, and know that He Is God. Exalt His name amongst the unbeliever because they will refuse to understand the reasoning for your praises.

Change your ways of thinking and be not conformed to the values and principles of the world. But meditate on God's Word and let the Holy Ghost transform your mind to prove what is good, acceptable, and perfect, will of God. Behave according to the biblical ordinances of righteousness. Behave not as the world. There must be a saving change wrought in you because Transformation and sanctification is the renewing of the mind. Renewing the mind shows affection for the will of God. Hence, the evidence, understanding, and attentiveness to Obedience will flourish in due season. Continue keeping your heart with all diligence; the issues of life flow from the heart. It is full of the burdens and troublesome affairs of life, so learn to transform it. Do not fashion yourself according to secular values. Sincerely, use all heavenly blessings entrusted to you to redirect your path. The outward man perishes by dying daily to lustful desires. Outward appearance is what can be seen by others. It resembles change, and the appearance of the inward man is renewed daily with the Holy Ghost.

Put On the New Man

In knowledge, we have by profession betrayed sin and gained Jesus Christ. Putting off the old man – says you are no longer conformed to the deeds of the flesh. Putting on the new man – says you have gained knowledge of the principles of holiness and righteousness. We are made after the image of Jesus Christ. Renew this mind not by works of righteousness, but according to God's mercies. He saved you by restoration, renewing of the Holy Ghost.

Come On Up To Mount Sinai
Exodus 34; Exodus 34; 2 Corinthians 3; Romans 8

In the morning, rise to meet Jesus Christ, we must be willing to come up higher, access the realm of the Holy of Holies to commune with him. We must be willing to go into the inner sanctuary of the Tabernacle where God's presence appears. Be Ready In The Morning. Your Vision Is clearer to go up in the morning to Mount Sinai and present yourself to The LORD Jesus Christ. There, "You Can RECEIVE" Revelation and Power, Instruction and Wisdom, find your purpose, Jesus Christ will allow you to "Shine." Your purpose-driven vision is clearer In Mount Sinai. There you can - enjoy the presence of God's Glory. Look out far beyond current circumstances and find yourself in the Living God. Resting in the Comfort zone of peace and tranquility. Listen and Commune with Jesus Christ.

In Mount Sinai, God instructed and hewed two tables of stone to write upon the heart and mind. He carves it out and embeds his Word and Testimonies. The crying heard is the voice of many that have turned away from serving a Mighty God! Something Happened that steered God's people from serving him. Troubles and Circumstances causes us to break the commandments of God. Let nothing separate you from the love of God, which is in Christ Jesus, our Lord.

When you come up to Mount Sinai –Jesus Christ will begin to engrave his commandments. The same commandments, WHICH WERE BROKEN from generation to generation. You Are A declared Epistle of Christ – wearing the letters of righteousness for all to see both verbal and written testimonies are evident in your life.

Come up alone to the place where Jesus Christ desires to meet and commune with you.

When you decide to come up to Mount Sinai, No one should come with you because the meetings on top of Mount Sinai are private moments Face to face, One on One. So, this is your year, and you have the power to make it a new beginning. Come On Up To Mount Sinai to speak with the Lord.

Listen, Hear ye, Hear ye

Hear What The Word Has To Say

Psalm 19

Don't Mess With the Recipe. It is perfect, transforming souls, it tells of the testimonies of Jesus Christ, which is sure and gives simple understanding. The law has its authority and all its excellency from the law-maker.

Testify About The Word of God and let everyone know; his Word gives the whole divine revelation, and it gives precepts (teachings, principles, and guidelines). God's Word promises it will never falter. Your heart rejoices and holds true to his statutes. The righteous rejoice in their heart because His commandments are pure and enlightens the eyes. We are no longer blind, but now we can see the victories won.

His Word is pure; every word is true. It cleanses and reaches deeply into the reign in the heart, removing guile, treachery, cunning, and filthiness; these are not linked to holiness. Practice every commandment, and patiently wait. Wait for the Holy Ghost to cleanse your temple. Jesus Christ is the Word, and it is good, sweeter than honey. There's A Great Reward in keeping and remaining obedient to the commandments. The Word makes you clean. Only the LORD can understand your errors, and in secret, he cleanses and washes away all your sins. Stand tall and solid.

Keep away from the arrogance of sins—do not sin just because you believe you can. Instead, seek the LORD and ask him to keep you from presumptuous sins and let them not have dominion over your life. Let the words of your mouth and the mediation of your heart, be acceptable in the sight of the LORD. He knows all things because He is a God the knows all things.

Yesterday

Yesterday, I sat in my favorite place, where I spoke with my Lord and Savior, Jesus Christ. I wasn't there too long—when my eyes begin to fill with tears, and I sat there and cried. In his presence, I cried. Loneliness filled my favorite spot, and it was no longer about being alone; but, more about being thankful. Jesus had always taken care of me, and when I thought he was not listening; he was still there leading and directing my path. At times, it felt as if my eyes were spiritually closed. I wanted to see what the Holy Ghost saw in me and how God had shifted things around to heal, deliver, and set me free. Sometimes, as I walked, I felt like a ping-pong ball bumping into objects ignoring the warning signs. Amid everything, it seemed nothing mattered because I knew Jesus Christ has always been so good to me.

When trouble showed up, He shielded my mind, heart, and soul. Although, my body ached with pain and heart filled with sorrow; He taught me to stand with boldness. His Spirit gave me strength, dictated my steps, and governed my world. He sent his messenger to say utterly—

> Stand tall, my child, even when the wind is blowing so hard, and you want to fall; stand tall. Look straight ahead, do not waver in your strength; instead, stand up and close your eyes. I will protect you, and you will never be alone. The days will feel empty; people laugh with you for a short time, but I give you joy for a lifetime. The love shared by the world could never compare to the love I have for you. So, let them all laugh, throw rocks, and shatter your dreams. Possibly, many will believe you are weak and fragile. Believe in my power, glory, and honor, and it will take you higher than you could ever imagine.

> The days, you feel no one cares, is the days of polishing the relationship built in me. Trust in me, and I will never leave you alone to fight many battles. I will give you the joy to replace the tears and boldness to stand in the face of fear.

The world is full of lions and wolves waiting to destroy your purpose; but, I am the author and finisher of your faith; depend on the guidance of the Holy Ghost to get you over and through.

In the mornings, look up in the sky, close your eyes, and allow my morning glory to shine upon your face. Feel the warmth of my love, worship me, acknowledge the new day created for my people, those who are called by my name. You have dug deep, found me, and treasured all my words of encouragement. They are written to teach my children how to fight using their whole hearts by learning to toss every conflict to me and allowing me to crush their enemies.

You are obligated to shower me with praise and call on my name daily to keep open the lines of communication. Each time you call me, I promise to hear, for my word will never return to me void, and it is the covenant I vowed with past and future generations. You will never find a God, such as I, one who loves unconditionally and delivers on every promise made. When your eyes feel with tears, you can lean on my shoulder and tell me all about the struggles. As you have said to me in more ways than one, the struggle is real. I understand how deep the wounds have buried in your life; but, I can dig deeper and uproot everything, not according to my plans.

Now, the time has come for you too look at me for everything and lean not into your understanding. Flip the pages of the Bible, share with me what you have read, and I will reveal unto you more wisdom, knowledge, and understanding. I want you to become prepared for the oracles you will speak to my Children. As the messenger, talk about the truth and say what you are directed to say; nothing more or less. For, I am the LORD your God. The same, yesterday, today, and forever.

Yesterday was yesterday. I created her and wrote about my people. Let not your mind focus on the things of yesterday. It is best to focus on today, the here, and now. Tomorrow, today will be known as yesterday, and I will continue to carry you as long as you keep to abide in me, and I will abide in you. I am your God the Holy One of Israel, your Savior; I gave Egypt for your ransom, Ethiopia, and Seba for you. There is nothing impossible for them who love me.

Trust in me, and I will lead you as far into VICTORY!

Winning against the Odds
Deuteronomy 20: 1-4; Isaiah 41:10; Ephesians 6:13; Ephesians 6:14-18; Ecclesiastes 5:1; Proverbs 4:27

We had received instructions given unto The Children of Israel when they were considered a Camp and Not a Kingdom. We are already in the midst of the Enemy's Territory. Often, God would give his servant a Word to encourage His flock.

Pick up Your Sword, which is the Word of God. Daily we are in a constant battle for our salvation. Consequently, we encounter a diverse set of people that has allowed unclean spirits to overtake them. We must always be girded with the Word of God, Armed for battle, and ready for war.

Do not be intimidated by the size of the problem. On the contrary, look at the size of your God. With Him, size does not matter. When warring against the enemy, oppressed by vicious militants, surrounding your camp, do you dare to be afraid? Jesus Christ is there, leading you to greener pastures to feast upon till your soul is full of the Manna, the bread which the Lord has given you to eat. The same God, which brought you up out of the land of Egypt. The place of bondage, whereas you were not able to breathe because elements of life were proven detrimental to your faith in God.

Encourage One Another

Do not become so eager for empty promises spoken by man. Their words do not have value, sounding like tinkling brass on a shivering cold night. Gird your loins with the strength given by the Holy Ghost. Be Not Afraid of Them, the uncircumcised who appears to intimidate your existence. Do you feel like running? Where would you run, and for what reason? Know that, "...The LORD, your God, is with you. His Presence is marrow to the bone and comfort to the heart, body, and soul. Encourage one another to seek the LORD, our God in great sincerity, and cease not to pray.

Winning against the Odds is to proclaim victory when it appears from different angles as sheer defeat. Willpower and determination deeply send shock waves to shake the core of your faith; forces you to learn Jesus will never leave your side. It was the same "LORD" that liberated you; during bondage, imprisonment, oppression, burdens, worries, and etcetera. Always be ready for a battle, fear not the issue, and never doubt The LORD your God.

Beneficial Factors

Why are you afraid? While you are lurking in the shadows of fear, Jesus Christ is near. Why are you disappointed with the charades of deceit and anguish? From the beginning, Jesus Christ has shown up on the scene to deliver, heal, set free, performing miracles which many still cannot believe. He strengthens areas, whereas we are weak and gave the Holy Ghost to help. Why flutter with misconceptions and false sayings; Jesus Christ will hold you up with his right hand of righteousness. Keep fighting and winning against the odds. When victory is prevalent, many will despise and others may rejoice in the positions provided to stand tall.

There will come a time when you might appear outnumbered but do not become apprehended or overwhelmed by the situation or circumstance. At times, we may not wrestle against the corrupt nature of humanity or their wickedness; but against the familiar spirit operating in their life. Keep your mind resting on the biblical principles of holiness and sanctification. Train your mind to rest in the presence of God because an unstable soul can become easily persuaded by ungodly events.

Stand

It takes a lot of strength to fight and a lot of hard work to stand. Jesus Christ is the Captain of our salvation, and he chooses to speak unto his people. In reality, ships have captains, airplanes have captains, and the military have captains. These are the Valor or Brave men and women in charge armed with authority, power and courage. In the midst of chaos, they are purposed to give Words of Encouragement to strengthen the hands of the people, and they lie to minimize fear.

Jesus Christ is the true Captain. He encourages his flock to stand and see the salvation of the LORD. God is not a man, that he should lie; neither the son of man, that he should repent. Has he said it, should he not do it? Or has he spoken, and should he not make it good?

Hear What The LORD Says

Let your Faith, Belief, and Confidence be in the Power of God. Let him fill your hearts. In the face of adversity, God Will take care of you. Let not your hearts faint and do not grow weak. Instead, continue to travail in your faith and put on your armor. Stand allowing the inward parts of your heart to be filled with the Gospel of Truth. Arm yourself with the breastplate of righteousness in Jesus Christ and have your Feet with the preparation of the gospel of peace and defend your position – restrain yourself to keep the peace. Take the shield of faith to quench or put out all the fiery, violent, cruel, and aggressive darts of the wicked. In the house of God, be ready to hear because obedience is better than any sacrifice offered. Turn not to the right hand nor to the left. Win against the odds by praying always with all prayer and supplication in the Holy Ghost, and remain watchful with all perseverance and supplication. God's people are the winners pushing against the odds.

Realize versus Spiritualize

Trying to find you deep within yourself, it is hard. Where do you begin and how do you start the search. Forced smiles, pretending all is well, faking the act, shaking and slapping yourself back into reality. The battles have shaken your foundation a little. After realizing what is going on, you slowly make moves to trick the adversary. The HOLY GHOST provides all the ways of escape and lets you know to stand in the presence of God, and His glory makes you invincible to the tactics of the enemy.

Hence, you plant your feet deeply in the trenches of the HOLY GHOST. As the winds bolster around and interfere with the atmospheric tensions of reality, you can take a deep breath and exhale. Finally, you have spiritualized and understand every fight is not your fight. Step back, look up, and run behind the skirt-tail of your Master, Lord, and Savior Jesus Christ. He has the power to cease every storm, shelter his people from the wiles of the devil, walk by mountains and rent them, and walk upon stumbling blocks crushing them to powder.

These are things we know to be true; when no one else believes, God's Children must trust. Trust in things we do not see, yet believing in the heart. He will never leave us naked, broken, and ashamed. Jesus will always ensure His people are well dressed in the richness of apparel. For whatever reason, we continuously fall short on all ends of the spectrum. If everything is going fine, we forget to thank Him for helping us overcome the barriers of defeat. Even when we do remember, is the gratitude sincere, or did we simply let the words roll from our lips to say, "we did thank Him."

Not so, Friend! When you look around and realize all is well and the battles have ceased, spiritualize this one thing, "God has given you peace."

Wars are not brewing in your mind to confuse it.
Wars are not instigating on the job to entice you.
Wars are not plotting in the home to overthrow you.

The LORD, in the magnitude of His Greatness, shares with us simple gifts. He knows too much of His goodness will cause us to revert to old habits, entangling ourselves again with bondage. Thus, He bathes us in simple gifts from the Holy Ghost. Each gift rejuvenates our vision, prepares the heart, and opens our ears to hear. The pouring of the oil upon the head anoints it to retain Wisdom. Gifts from the Holy Ghost makes us rich and adds no sorrow. With gladness, the simplicity which lies within peace, tranquility, and serenity can rest on our hearts and feed us the heavenly Manna, which rains from the skies. The adversary does not have the power to confiscate your peace unless it is granted unto him.

For these reasons, our sacrificial offering should resemble nothing but WORSHIP IN THE BEAUTY OF HOLINESS. In this world, we cannot and will not survive without the covering of the Blood of Jesus Christ. After realizing, the peace that you have and trouble is found nowhere, not even around the corners of despair. Spiritualize your faith to strengthen its foundation. Read, meditate, and study the precepts of God's promises. Spend time in perfecting your weapons of destruction against the enemy, which is your relationship in Jesus Christ.

Released November 14, 2018

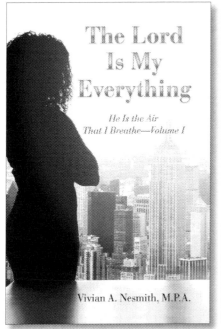 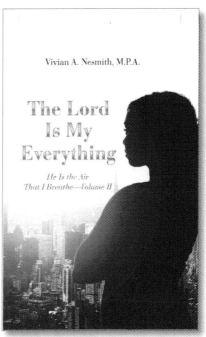

New Book Release:
From Boot Camp to The Pulpit

The Lord Is My Everything "He Is The
Air That I Breathe" – Volume III

You may purchase these book titles on:
https://www.westbowpress.com/en/bookstore

Or Visit My Website:
https://nesmithassociatesincorporated.com/